THE
CONDITIONING
THERAPIES

Contributors

ARTHUR J. BACHRACH
Professor and Chairman, Department of Psychology,
Arizona State University

PERCIVAL BAILEY
Director of Research, Illinois State Psychiatric Institute

HERVEY M. CLECKLEY
Clinical Professor of Psychiatry
Department of Neurology and Psychiatry,
Medical College of Georgia

CYRIL M. FRANKS
Director of the Psychological Service
and Research Center, New Jersey Neuropsychiatric Institute

W. HORSLEY GANTT
Professor Emeritus of Psychiatry
and Director of the Pavlovian Laboratory,
Johns Hopkins University School of Medicine

A. HUSSAIN
Psychiatrist, Harlem Valley State Hospital, Wingdale, New York

PETER J. LANG
Associate Professor of Psychology,
Department of Psychology, University of Wisconsin

HOWARD S. LIDDELL
Late Professor of Psychobiology
and Director of the Behavior Farm Laboratory, Cornell University

L. J. REYNA
Professor of Psychology
Department of Psychology, Boston University

ANDREW SALTER
Consulting Psychologist, New York City

CORBETT H. THIGPEN
Associate Clinical Professor of Psychiatry,
Department of Neurology and Psychiatry,
Medical College of Georgia

JOSEPH WOLPE
Professor of Psychiatry, Department of Neurology and Psychiatry,
University of Virginia School of Medicine

THE
CONDITIONING
THERAPIES

The Challenge in Psychotherapy

EDITED BY

Joseph Wolpe, M. D.

UNIVERSITY OF VIRGINIA SCHOOL OF MEDICINE

Andrew Salter

NEW YORK CITY

L. J. Reyna, Ph. D.

BOSTON UNIVERSITY

Holt, Rinehart and Winston, Inc.

New York · *Chicago* · *San Francisco* · *Toronto* · *London*

Preface

The University of Virginia Conference, which this book reports, was intended to call the attention of the interested professions to the growing strength of the behavioristic position in psychotherapy. But since the psychoanalytic (or "psychodynamic") schools dominate psychotherapy today, the conference became *ipso facto* a public challenge to them.

To issue a challenge is to declare the essentials of a case, and not to argue the case in detail. It is seldom possible for a conference to provide the systematic elaboration of an argument, and this conference was no exception. It was, in fact, like most conferences: the papers had a pattern of integration, but essentially presented a patchwork of topics that left large areas untouched. Yet this patchwork turned out to be exciting, and as provocative as a challenge should be.

In preparing the transcript we have tried to retain the flavor of the conference, while largely removing the repetitive and discursive quality that makes most conference proceedings so difficult to read. In this endeavor we have had the full collaboration of the authors.

The "conditioning therapies," or as they are also called, "behavior therapy," are an endorsement of the medical axiom that understanding the pathological begins with the study of physiology. The physiology of psychiatry consists of two parts—the biology of the nervous system, and the study of the factors that control its behavior—which is the domain of experimental psychology. The latter has been most relevant to the understanding of the neuroses and to the evolution of the conditioning therapies. A considerable and persuasive body of theory has grown up, and the clinical evidence of therapeutic effectiveness has been steadily accumulating.

The reader whose interest is aroused by the papers of the conference will probably want to acquaint himself with more explicit and detailed publications, many of which are mentioned in the references at the end of each chapter and in the annotated bibliography at the end of this book. Those who would like to be in touch with the active issues of the present time are directed to the recently established quarterly, *Behaviour Research and Therapy*—a journal that itself is a manifestation of the increasing development of the field—and the *Journal of Experimental Analysis of Behavior*.

Dr. Joseph Wolpe was conference chairman. We thank the other

faculty members of the University of Virginia who presided at the sessions
—Dr. William Parson of the Department of Internal Medicine, Dr. L.
Starling Reed of the Department of Psychology, and Dr. T. R. Johns of
the Department of Neurology and Psychiatry. In particular, we should
like to thank Dr. Ian Stevenson for his help and cooperation in making
this conference possible.

June 1964
Charlottesville, Virginia   J. W.
New York City, New York   A. S.
Boston, Massachusetts   L. J. R.

Contents

III *Associated Experimental Data*

IV *Prospects*

I

The Therapeutic Challenge

OPENING REMARKS

Ian Stevenson, M.D.

I think it is appropriate that a conference of this sort takes place at the University of Virginia, and I am delighted that it is being conducted under our auspices. So far as I know, although this is not a new kind of conference, it is a conference with a new kind of topic, and it could also be an extremely important conference.

I believe it is fair to say that for the past sixty years psychoanalytic therapy and psychoanalysis have been the dominant therapies in American, and to a considerable extent in European, psychiatry. It has been customary to contrast the possible benefits to the patient from psychoanalysis with what would be characterized, often despairingly, as supportive therapy—a kind of patching up of the patient—or with no therapy at all. For the most part, the psychoanalysts have had the discussion very much their own way, with relatively little challenge of their position that psychoanalysis was by far the best method of treatment, and the best course for the patient (certainly with psychoneurosis), to pursue.

Now I think three developments in the past fifteen years have radically changed the position. First, I believe, is the considerable criticism of the basis for the claims of the results of psychoanalytic therapy. A number of papers questioning the statistical validity and the criteria of improvement of psychoanalysts have been published in the past fifteen years and, on the whole, so far as I can tell, these criticisms have not been fairly met.

Second, we have had, in the last fifteen years, five independent studies of results in patients who are untreated, and a number of other studies in some depth of individual untreated patients, so that it has become quite clear that a patient with a psychoneurosis who does not receive treatment is not necessarily condemned to suffer for the rest of his life. Many of these patients get well within one to a few years, and, moreover, they get well quite substantially.

The third and most important development, however, is that which this conference will explore, mainly, the development of radical, new therapies, departing quite distinctly from the psychoanalytic techniques. I regard these new therapies as far more important than their concomitant theories, which I think have nothing whatever to do with the question of whether these new therapies are better than the old ones. And this, I think, is the challenge to psychoanalysis today.

Of these new forms of therapy, for which the claim is made that they are better than no treatment and better than supportive treatment, and also better than psychoanalysis, I would like to say, however, that I think there is also an important challenge to the challengers, and I take it that this exists in two aspects. The first questions that I think we are entitled to ask are, Will the studies and the investigations that are presented by the challengers be based on better methods, and on more rigorous and more disciplined thinking? Will their criteria of improvement be more accurately defined and their methods be more replicable?

And the second challenge to them is—and here I think we have an even more serious and difficult challenge—Can they avoid partisanship? Can they dissect issues, and separate out practice from theory and from individual items of practice, or will there be further calls to subscribe to whole systems? If these two criteria are not met by the challengers, I'm afraid we are all going to become very bored and angry, because we will feel we have been through it once before—not we personally, but our predecessors fifty years ago who listened to the psychoanalysts as they were rising. I myself am convinced that this is not going to happen, and that we are about to hear testimony to a challenge that is well based and very well worth paying attention to.

THE COMPARATIVE CLINICAL STATUS
OF CONDITIONING THERAPIES
AND PSYCHOANALYSIS

Joseph Wolpe, M.D.

The germinal cause of the convocation of this conference is the presence of a vast problem: how to lift the burden of suffering that neurosis imposes on humanity. The foremost task of the clinician is always the relief of suffering, and his effectiveness in accomplishing it depends upon the potency of the methods he uses.

Whatever the problem at issue, the clinical status of a method, or of a principle that generates methods, is, or should be, assessed on several criteria. The primary criteria relate directly to the well-being of the patient. Is the suffering alleviated? If so, how quickly, how completely, and how enduringly? And how free is the accomplishment from disadvantageous sequelae? Secondary criteria are the amount of time and effort demanded of the therapist, and the cost of the treatment to the patient.

Let us scrutinize the application to the neuroses of the primary criteria of the clinical status of treatments. Almost invariably, what motivates the patient to come to us in the first place is the presence of various kinds of suffering and disability, which frequently, on investigating his case, we may find even more widespread than he may initially have been able to verbalize. It is both inevitable and reasonable that the patient will ultimately appraise his therapy in terms of the relief that he will experience—just as he would if his suffering were due to an organic disease. The indispensability of this yardstick is recognized by anybody with a medical background, and the different aspects of it were very helpfully systematized by Knight (1941) when he proposed his criteria

5

for evaluating the outcome of psychoanalytic therapy. The criteria he put forth were five—symptomatic improvement, increased productiveness, improved adjustment and pleasure in sex, improved interpersonal relationships, and ability to handle ordinary psychological conflicts and reasonable reality stresses. Every treated case can be assessed with these criteria in mind. But it is important to realize that only one of them is *always* relevant, and that is symptomatic improvement, because neuroses vary with regard to interference with functions. For example, a man with neurotic anxieties in group situations may have a completely satisfying sex life, and a man with sexual anxieties may be productive and happy at work and altogether at ease in social situations.

Having said that symptomatic improvement is the only criterion of improvement of neuroses that must be taken into account in every case, I must make my meaning clear. Baldly stated, symptomatic improvement simply means that the patient has less discomfort. Discomfort can be diminished in a variety of ways. One method consists of the use of appropriate drugs. Although drugs are a valuable *aid* to treatment of many cases, for several reasons it is unsatisfactory to base treatment solely on them. The alleviation of symptoms is often only partial, there may be side effects, there are risks of toxicity and addiction, and, above all, the need for treatment may well continue indefinitely. Psychoanalysts and conditioning therapists are at one in comparing this with treating a slipped spinal disc with analgesics; they rightly disparage it, favoring the superior therapeutic objective of removing the underlying state of affairs upon which the symptoms depend. In other words, they both advocate aiming at a *radical* cure of neurosis, to render the patient free from his symptoms without the use of drugs or other means of palliation. Among other palliative measures I include taking the patient away from a disturbing environment, or manipulating the environment so as to ameliorate stressful features. Clearly, if the underlying basis of his symptoms were to be removed, the patient would be symptom-free without drugs in all circumstances in which symptoms were previously evoked. The crucial question, then, in comparing the clinical status of the conditioning therapies with that of psychoanalysis is: how effective is each of them in achieving this result?

While directing our minds to this practical question, we must be aware that at bottom the conflict is one of *concepts*. The comparison is not between this and that batch of methods that are merely empirically different, like some of the remedies for warts, but between two different conceptions of the nature of neurosis, each of which generates methods of treatment consistent with it. The different theories of neurosis suggest different requirements for recovery, and therefore different therapeutic maneuvers. In carrying out appropriate therapeutic maneuvers one is in fact performing operations that test predictions from the respective theories. As always in science, a theory becomes questionable when its predictions fail to be supported by experience.

PSYCHOANALYTIC THERAPY

With the foregoing as orientation we may proceed to evaluate the clinical status of psychoanalytic therapy. The conception of neurotic symptoms that leads to this therapy is that they are the consequences of emotional forces that have been repressed, taking the form of compromises between partial discharges of these forces and various defenses resisting their discharge. In 1922 Freud put it in the following words:

> The neuroses are the expression of conflicts between the ego and such of the sexual impulses as seem to the ego incompatible with its integrity or with its ethical standards. . . . Symptoms are in the nature of compromise-formations between the repressed sexual instincts and the repressive ego instincts. . . .

Although some analysts may protest that this statement is out of date, modern deviators from Freud, such as Horney, Fromm, and Alexander, differ from him mainly in the direction of ascribing greater importance to unconscious conflicts related to the immediate situation of the patient. The core of the theory remains, and with it, quite naturally, a broad basis of agreement upon what needs to be done in therapy, this being a logical deduction from the theory. The psychoanalytic objective is to overcome a neurosis by making repressed impulses conscious, using various tactics to overcome the resistances that oppose this. Munroe (1955) has said that the crux of the therapeutic process not only for Freud, but also for Adler, Horney, Fromm, and Sullivan "may be stated as the development of insight," not mere intellectual insight, but "the actual *experiencing* of aspects of one's personality which have been made defensively unconscious." This whole matter has been discussed more fully in another context (Wolpe, 1961a).

We need to consider to what extent the therapeutic procedures based on psychoanalytic theory have been effective in bringing about recovery from neurosis. It must be said at once that the evidence available is remarkable for its paucity, considering that psychoanalysis has been practiced for sixty years. It is also remarkable that, as far as I have been able to discover, not a single individual psychoanalyst has ever published a statistical survey of his own practice. Is it unreasonable to ask if this may be at least partly because they have not been very happy with their results?

In respect to those results that have been published, we are constantly faced with the problem whether or not, in assessing a case as improved, criteria such as Knight's have been applied by the analyst. I have again and again seen cases claimed as successes of analytic psychotherapy that would certainly be rated failures on Knight's criteria. For example, a young woman's analysis by a Freudian analyst was terminated despite only slight diminution of severe interpersonal anxiety reactions on the grounds that she had graduated to "emotional maturity," and that her dreams had changed. In another case, a Sullivan-oriented therapist discharged as recovered a man with marked anxiety reactions to aggressive behavior of others, on the criterion that the patient "now fully accepts himself and his reactions," even though the anxiety reactions were as strong as ever. That at least some analysts should favorably evaluate such outcomes need not surprise us when we consider the criteria they themselves set for terminating a psychoanalysis. The criteria used by a number of analysts were given by Wilder in his famous paper, "Facts and Figures on Psychotherapy" (1945). The criteria most frequently stated by the analysts were "the patient's ability to accept freely his sexuality, freedom in social relations and freedom from disturbance in work." Other criteria were insight, acceptance of heterosexuality, solution of the internal conflict, receding of childhood transference, substantial working through of the Oedipus constellation, and freedom from symptoms. Wilder's comment is, "It is interesting to note that freedom from symptoms as a criterion plays a minor role."

It seems fair to conclude that, in at least some cases judged by psychoanalysts as recovered, Knight's criteria are not complied with, and there is not the relief from suffering that is our main interest here. However, this need not deflect us from the comparison we wish to make. We can be generous and suppose that, by and large, where recovery has been claimed, Knight's criteria *would have been* satisfied.

The older statistical studies were tabulated in 1941 by Knight. They comprise reports from the Berlin Psychoanalytic Institute, the Chicago Psychoanalytic Institute, the Menninger Clinic, the London Psychoanalytic Clinic, and a small group of cases reported by Kessel and Hyman. Out of a total of 534 cases listed as "psychoneuroses," 242 were either apparently cured or much improved. This is a success rate of 45 percent of the total number of patients, and 63.2 percent if patients who had less than six months of therapy are excluded (Table 1, p. 14). Knight himself remarked that those thus excluded "represent an important group of failures."

For many years no further statistical data were published. However, a few years ago, the American Psychoanalytic Association appointed its now famous Fact-Gathering Committee to survey the results of psychoanalytic practice. The chairman of this committee, Dr. Harry I. Weinstock, subsequently stated at a lecture at the Maudsley Hospital, London, that his association made *no claims of therapeutic usefulness for psychoanalytic methods* (Eysenck, 1960). In March 1962, Dr. Morris W. Brody, of Temple University, revealed some details (Brody, 1962). (See also Masserman, 1963.) Of 595 patients who undertook analysis, 306 were regarded as having been "completely analyzed." Of the latter number, 210 were followed up after completing their analyses, and 126 of them, or 60 percent, were stated to have been cured or greatly improved. This percentage is not much more than would be expected of simple traditional therapy (Wilder, 1945), but when one looks more closely the picture is even less impressive. If the percentage of favorable results is viewed with reference to the total number of patients treated by the analysts (and not only those "completely analyzed"), the success rate is less (see Table 1). Alternatively, considering only the completely analyzed cases, it seems to be a controversion of the psychoanalytic theory of neurosis if 40 percent of the analyses that were rated complete did not effect marked improvement, let alone complete recovery. If that theory accorded with reality, would not "complete analysis" remove the whole basis of the patient's neurosis?

But even at the figure of 60 percent apparently cured or much improved—even then, as Wilder noted, the results do not show any definite superiority over the results obtained in hospitals or clinics or by psychotherapists employing the various conventional methods. The fact that so much effort, more than 600 hours (Masserman, 1963) for each markedly improved case in the series, was needed to produce such undistinguished results raises the startling question whether psychoanalytic therapy introduces features into therapy that actually impede recovery!

THE CONDITIONING THERAPIES

Now let us consider the conditioning therapies. These methods stem from the conception that neuroses are persistent unadaptive habits that have been conditioned (that is, learned). If this conception is correct, the fundamental overcoming of a neurosis *can* consist of nothing but deconditioning—or undoing the relevant habit patterns.

The most characteristic and common feature of neurotic habits is anxiety. There is persuasive evidence, both experimental and clinical,

that the great majority of neuroses are fundamentally conditioned autonomic responses (Wolpe, 1958). The individual has persistent habits of
reacting with anxiety to situations that, objectively, are not dangerous.
Typical stimuli to which the response of anxiety may be regarded as
neurotic are the sight of a bird, the interior of an elevator, asking a favor,
or receiving a compliment. Experimentally it is possible to condition an
animal to respond with anxiety to any stimulus one pleases merely by
arranging for that stimulus, on a number of occasions, to appear in an
appropriate time relation to the evocation of anxiety; and by manipulating various factors one can obtain an emotional habit that is utterly
refractory to extinction in the ordinary way (Wolpe, 1948, 1958). In
human neuroses one can usually elicit a history of similar kinds of conditioning. Human neuroses, too, are characterized by the same remarkable resistance to extinction. Since neurotic reactions are, as a rule,
autonomic reactions first and foremost, this resistance is in keeping with
Gantt's observations of the great refractoriness of cardiovascular conditioned responses to extinction (p. 121).

It is implicit in conditioning theory that recovery from neurosis should
be achieved by applying the learning process in a reverse direction:
whatever undesirable behavior has been learned may be unlearned. In
experiments performed about fourteen years ago I demonstrated in cats
that had been made neurotic experimentally how this unlearning can be
brought about (Wolpe, 1948, 1958). Anxiety reactions had been strongly
conditioned to a small confining cage and to other stimuli, and could not
be made to extinguish despite repeated exposure to the stimuli. The
anxiety response habits could, however, be overcome in piecemeal fashion
by counterposing feeding to weak anxiety responses. At first, stimuli
distantly similar to the conditioned stimuli were used, until anxiety de-
creased to zero, and then, step by step, stimuli closer in resemblance
to the original conditioned stimuli were introduced, until even the strongest
eventually lost its power to evoke anxiety. These findings led to the
framing of the reciprocal inhibition principle of psychotherapy, which is
that *if a response inhibitory of anxiety can be made to occur in the
presence of anxiety-evoking stimuli it will weaken the bond between these
stimuli and the anxiety.*

Experience with human neuroses indicates that the principle has
quite general validity; in addition to feeding, a good many other kinds
of responses,[1] each of which, empirically, appears to inhibit anxiety, have
been successfully used to weaken neurotic anxiety-response habits and

---

[1] Gellhorn and Loofbourrow (1963) present a number of modern instances of
reciprocally inhibitory relationships between reactions in both the somatic and
the autonomic nervous systems. (See also Gellhorn, 1961.)

related neurotic habits. The reciprocal inhibition principle also affords an explanation for the therapeutic effects of interviewing as such (which is seemingly the main basis of the successes of the traditional therapies) and for so-called spontaneous recoveries.

I have described elsewhere (1958) the deliberate therapeutic use of a considerable range of anxiety-inhibiting responses. I shall briefly review those most widely employed—assertive, relaxation, and sexual responses.

Assertive responses are used where there is a need to overcome neurotic anxieties that arise irrationally in the course of interpersonal relationships—such anxieties as prevent a person from expressing his opinions to his friends lest they disagree, or from reprimanding inefficient underlings. The essence of the therapist's role is to encourage appropriate assertiveness, the outward expression, wherever it is reasonable and right to do so, of the feelings and action tendencies that anxiety has in the past inhibited. In other words, the therapist instigates "acting out." Each act of assertion to some extent reciprocally inhibits the anxiety, and in consequence somewhat weakens the anxiety response habit. The assertion required is not necessarily aggressive, and behavior in accordance with affectionate and other feelings may need to be instigated. The maneuvers involved are largely similar to those described by Salter (1949), though the rationale upon which he bases them is different.

Relaxation responses were first used on a scientific basis by Jacobson (1939), who demonstrated that they have autonomic accompaniments opposite to those of anxiety. His method of intensive training in relaxation for use in the life situation, though of great value, is rather cumbersome. More economical and clearly directed use of relaxation is made in the technique known as *systematic desensitization* (Wolpe, 1958, 1961b).

Lang reports its use in the context of snake phobias,[2] but its range of application is very wide indeed.[3] The therapist has to identify the categories of stimuli to which the patient reacts with anxiety, and then rank the stimuli of each category in order of intensity of evoked anxiety. In the course of about six interviews the patient is given training in relaxation in parallel with this. When the preliminaries have been com-

---

[2] See pages 38–49.

[3] Some people are erroneously under the impression that this method is effective only for classical phobias. The word "phobia" refers to clearly defined stimulus sources of neurotic anxiety. The conditioning therapist differs from his colleagues in that he *seeks out* the precise stimuli to anxiety, and finds himself able to break down almost every neurosis into what are essentially *phobic systems*. Their subject matter extends far beyond the classical phobias, and includes such contents as neurotic fears of incurring obligations, of being watched, or of receiving praise. (See Wolpe, 1964.)

pleted, the patient is made to relax as deeply as possible (in some cases under hypnosis), and then instructed to imagine the weakest of the anxiety-evoking stimuli for a few seconds. The instruction is repeated at short intervals, and if the response to the stimulus has been weak initially, it declines, on repetition, to zero. Under these circumstances, what apparently happens is that on each occasion the relaxation inhibits the anxiety, to some extent, and somewhat weakens the anxiety-evoking potential of the stimulus concerned. With repetition this potential is brought down to zero.

Recent studies have demonstrated:

—that the effects of desensitization are due to the procedure itself and not to suggestion or transference (Wolpe, 1962; Lang, pp. 47–48);

—that after one or two sessions it can be predicted with virtual certainty whether a patient will respond to this treatment or not; and

—that in phobias with independently measurable parameters, such as acrophobia, the numbers of therapeutic operations involved show consistent mathematical relationships to the stages of decrement of the phobia (Wolpe, 1963) that are suggestively similar to the psychophysical law proposed by Stevens (1962).

Sexual responses are used to inhibit anxiety responses conditioned to sexual situations. By manipulating the conditions of sexual approaches so that anxiety is never permitted to be strong, reciprocal inhibition of anxiety by sexual arousal is effected, and the anxiety response habit is progressively weakened. It is usually possible to overcome impotence or premature ejaculation in a few weeks. Sexual responses have generally only a secondary role in the treatment of frigidity (Lazarus, 1963b).

The question is, how effective are these and related techniques in procuring the recovery of neurotic patients in terms of Knight's criteria?

Using the whole range of available methods according to their indications, I have reported between 1952 and 1958 three series of results embracing 210 neurotic patients. Every patient in whom the reciprocal inhibition techniques had been given a fair trial was included in the series. Nearly 90 percent of these patients were rated on Knight's criteria as either apparently cured or much improved after an average of about 30 therapeutic interviews. The cases were unselected in the sense that no case diagnosed as neurotic was ever refused treatment. Psychotics and psychopaths were not accepted for treatment unless by error of diagnosis.

Until recently, there were no other studies involving considerable numbers of patients, although numerous accounts had been published describing the successful treatment of individuals or small groups. One noteworthy small group comprised 18 cases of phobias in children treated by Lazarus (1959). All the patients recovered in a mean of 9.5 sessions; follow-up from six months to two and a half years showed no relapses. Lazarus has recently analyzed his results with reciprocal inhibition therapies. His findings[4] have been summarized in a mimeographed paper as follows: In the course of about 4 years the *total* number of patients who consulted him was 408. Of these, 321 (or 78 percent) derived "definite and constructive benefit according to certain specified criteria which are unusually stringent." Hussain reports[5] 95 percent of 105 patients whom he treated by a direct approach involving hypnosis apparently recovered or much improved. Recently, I received from the Hospital for Mental and Nervous Diseases at St. John's, Newfoundland, a report by Drs. Alastair Burnett and Edmond Ryan of the treatment of 100 neurotic patients on learning theory principles. The usual treatment period was five weeks. The evaluation of outcome was on Knight's criteria. Substantial improvement occurred in almost every case (Burnett, 1962). Twenty-five of the patients were followed up over a year or more, and fifteen of these (60 percent) were then either apparently cured or much improved. Another 32 percent were rated "moderately improved." As the outcome of five weeks of therapy this is quite noteworthy. Burnett and Ryan express the view that these methods make effective psychotherapy available for the first time to "fairly large numbers of rural, unsophisticated patients who have limited formal education."

In Table 1, the results of the two largest and most characteristic behavior therapy series are compared with those of the two major psychoanalytic series discussed above.

A critical question is, of course, the durability of the results obtained by conditioning methods. The answer appears to be that they are practically always long-lasting. In 1958 I was able to report only one relapse among forty-five patients who had been followed up for periods ranging from two to seven years. Published communication from other conditioning therapists indicates that their experience is essentially the same. Furthermore, whenever resurgence of symptoms has occurred, and could be investigated, it has always been found to be related to specific events that could clearly have reconditioned the neurotic emotional habit. Learning theory predicts that *unless* there are intervening events that directly recondition neurotic reactions, recovery from neurosis that is radical in the sense defined earlier in this paper will be lasting, no matter by what

---

[4] These have since been published (Lazarus, 1963a). See Table 1.
[5] See pages 54–61.

The Therapeutic Challenge

TABLE 1
Comparative Results

Series	No. of cases	Apparently cured or much improved (recoveries)	Percentage recoveries
Psychoanalytic Therapy			
Collected series of psychoneuroses (Knight, 1941)			
a. Over 6 months' therapy	383		63.2
		242	
b. Total cases	534		45.3
Psychoanalytic Fact-gathering Committee (Brody, 1962)	210	126	60
a. Completely analyzed cases	210	126	60
b. Total cases	595	(184)	(31)[a]
Behavior Therapy			
Wolpe (1958)	210	188	89.5[b]
Lazarus (1963)	408	321	78.0[b]

[a] This percentage is calculated from data of the Fact-Gathering Committee of the American Psychoanalytic Association, as follows. It is granted that the whole "completely analyzed" group of 306 would have shown the 60% recovery rate found in the 210 who were followed up, giving 184 recoveries for 306 patients. These would appear to be the sum total of patients claimed as apparently cured or much improved out of the whole group of 595, which includes 289 who discontinued analysis (Brody, 1962; Masserman, 1963).

[b] Lazarus included in his series *every* neurotic patient—even if he had seen him only once. Wolpe counted only those to whom the available techniques had actually been applied. When treatment was ineffective, this was generally established in 15–30 sessions.

maneuvers it has been obtained. There are facts that bear out this prediction. I elsewhere reported (Wolpe, 1961a) a survey of follow-up studies on neurotic patients who, with various therapies, other than psychoanalysis, had either recovered or improved markedly. Of 249 patients followed up from two to fifteen years only 4 had relapsed. This finding is not only in line with conditioning theory, but also directly contrary to the expectations of the psychoanalytic theory of neurosis.

CONCLUSIONS

The comparison I have presented is, of course, not based on data emanating from a controlled study on matched patients. Such a study, which should include an untreated group of patients similarly matched, is obviously desirable. Nevertheless, I submit that the evidence justifies now substituting behavior therapy for psychoanalysis in the training of therapists, and not temporizing until absolute proof has been provided. There are some who favor waiting for a study on matched groups of patients on the ground that the inferior results of psychoanalysis may be attributable to the psychoanalysts having to treat more difficult cases. There are several reasons for thinking this unlikely. In the first place, while conditioning therapists as a rule undertake treatment of all cases of neurosis, psychoanalysts are often very selective, and surely do not refuse those whom they believe they could *easily* help. Second, conditioning therapists frequently overcome neuroses that have been unsuccessfully treated by psychoanalysis, and often for many years. Third, in private practice, the individual medical practitioner tends to send *all* his neurotic cases to a favored psychotherapist, whether analyst or not. Fourth, it is at least tangentially relevant that, as already noted, psychoanalysts often profess a disinterest in symptomatic recovery, claiming that they aim at something "deeper," such as radical personality change. It may, however, be noted parenthetically that the analysts often represent this alleged deep kind of change as being *prerequisite* to durable freedom from symptoms, a proposition that evidence I have quoted flatly contradicts.

The present position is clear. As far as the evidence goes, conditioning therapies appear to produce a higher proportion of lasting recoveries from the distress and disability of neurosis than does psychoanalysis. Even if a controlled study were to show an equal, or even higher, percentage of recovery for psychoanalysis, the time it requires would remain incomparably greater, and conditioning therapy would therefore still deserve preference. The possible public health implications are great. A psychotherapist who uses behavioristic techniques can handle over ten times as many patients per year as the therapist who employs psychoanalysis, and with greater hope of success for each patient. Effective treatment has thus become possible for many more victims of neurotic disturbance—and at much less expense than psychoanalysis requires.

REFERENCES

BRODY, M. W. Prognosis and results of psychoanalysis. In J. H. Nodine and J. H. Moyer (Eds.), *Psychosomatic medicine*. Philadelphia: Lea & Febiger, 1962.

BURNETT, A. Personal communication, 1962.

BURNETT, A., & RYAN, E. *The outpatient treatment of neuroses by reciprocal inhibition methods.* In mimeograph, St. John's Hospital, Newfoundland, 1962.

EYSENCK, H. J. *Behaviour therapy and the neuroses.* New York: Pergamon, 1960.

FREUD, S. *Collected papers.* Vol. 5 London: Hogarth, 1950. (Encyclopedia article on psychoanalysis written in 1922)

GELLHORN, E. Prolegomena to a theory of emotions. *Perspec. Biol. Med.,* 1961, *4,* 403–436.

GELLHORN, E., & LOOFBOURROW, G. N. *Emotions and emotional disorders.* New York: Harper, 1963.

JACOBSON, E. *Progressive relaxation.* Chicago: U. Chicago Press, 1939.

KNIGHT, R. P. Evaluation of the results of psychoanalytic therapy. *Amer. J. Psychiat.,* 1941, *98,* 434–446.

LAZARUS, A. A. The elimination of children's phobias by deconditioning. *Med. Proc.,* 1959, *5,* 261–265.

LAZARUS, A. A. The results of behavior therapy in 126 cases of severe neurosis. *Behav. Res. Ther.* 1963, *1,* 69–80 (a).

LAZARUS, A. A. The treatment of chronic frigidity by systematic desensitization. *J. nerv. ment. Dis.* 1963, *136,* 272–278 (b).

MASSERMAN, J. H. Ethology, comparative biodynamics, and psychoanalytic research. In J. Scher (Ed.), *Theories of the mind.* New York: Free Press, 1963.

MUNROE, R. *Schools of psychoanalytic thought.* New York: Holt, Rinehart. and Winston, 1955.

SALTER, A. *Conditioned reflex therapy.* New York: Farrar, Straus, 1949, and Capricorn Books, Putnam's Sons, 1961.

STEVENS, S. S. The surprising simplicity of sensory metrics. *Amer. Psychol.,* 1962, *17,* 29–39.

WILDER, J. Facts and figures on psychotherapy. *J. clin. Psychopath.,* 1945, *7,* 311–347.

WOLPE, J. *An approach to the problem of neurosis based on the conditioned response.* M.D. thesis, University of the Witwatersrand, 1948.

WOLPE, J. *Psychotherapy by reciprocal inhibition.* Stanford: Stanford U. Press, 1958.

WOLPE, J. The prognosis in unpsychoanalyzed recovery from neurosis. *Amer. J. Psychiat.,* 1961, *117,* 35–39 (a).

WOLPE, J. The systematic desensitization treatment of neuroses. *J. nerv. ment. Dis.,* 1961, *132,* 189–203 (b).

WOLPE, J. Isolation of a conditioning procedure as the crucial psychotherapeutic factor. *J. nerv. ment. Dis.,* 1962, *134,* 316–329.

WOLPE, J. Quantitative relations in the systematic desensitization treatment of phobias. *Amer. J. Psychiat.,* 1963, *119,* 1062–1068.

WOLPE, J. Behavior therapy in complex neurotic states. *Brit. J. Psychiat.,* 1964, *110,* 28–34.

DISCUSSION

Stevenson: I would like to say something about the statistical comparison of psychotherapeutic results. It's entirely true, as Dr. Wolpe says, that there is a paucity of results published of psychotherapy by psycho-analysis. He's not quite right in saying that there are no reports of the results of individual psychoanalysts. I am going to mention the work of Scheldrup of Oslo with which you are apparently not acquainted. Scheldrup did report an analysis of some ten or twenty follow-ups of all his patients, and claimed that about two thirds of them were much improved or cured.

And also, despite Dr. Wolpe's contention, I must insist on our having matched control series before we subscribe wholeheartedly to any psychotherapeutics. How are we otherwise to know that, for example, Knight's criteria were really applied in the same way in Dr. Wolpe's series and in the Berlin psychoanalytic series? I don't see any way out of it, and we must be sure, also, I think, that the statistical methods were properly similar. Now, I don't think this is true of the comparison Dr. Wolpe makes between his series and that, for example, of the Berlin Psychoanalytic Institute. Dr. Wolpe compares his rate of recovery as much improved, 90 percent, with that of the Berlin Psychoanalytic Institute's 62 percent. But in Dr. Wolpe's book he indicates that certain patients who did not in his opinion have a thorough exposure to his program were not included in the final evaluation; and he lists at one point, 295 patients as having had Willoughby tests, which means that these patients must at least have got as far as this stage of evaluation, and, in a sense, had their intake examinations. Now, if we take his entire series amounting to at least 295 patients, and recalculate these data including these patients, then his results, over all, even accepting that he has used the same criteria, fall to 65 percent, and really are not any more 90 percent. I think this is an extremely important point. Let me close by saying I am extremely impressed by the results of Dr. Wolpe's methods and other behavioristic therapies in certain selected patients, but I remain on the fence with regard to their general application in all patients.

Wolpe: The issues that are raised here are important. Dr. Stevenson says that he must insist upon having a properly controlled comparative series. I agree with him that we should have such a comparison, but I do not think, in view of the facts already available, that we need wait for this to discard psychoanalysis and to make some changes. Dr. Stevenson fears that Knight's criteria may have been used differently by behaviorists and psychoanalysts, possibly creating a bias in favor of the behaviorists. These criteria are our yardstick. In the conditioning series, they are the very basis of evaluation. In the psychoanalytic series they were not deliberately applied. Therefore, the figures for favorable results of analysis must include many cases—like the two examples in my paper—that do not conform to these criteria. Their results would almost certainly look worse if we counted as successes only cases that improved on Knight's criteria. In any case, even if we were to find that the percentage of recoveries for psychoanalysis were as high as that for conditioning therapy, the latter would still be rated superior because of its far quicker results and its economy. I agree that we ought to have a controlled study, but we already have sufficient grounds to take action to improve the present unsatisfactory situation in psychotherapeutic practice.

The other point that I want to make relates to Dr. Stevenson's statement that in my book there is mention of 295 Willoughby scores. Quite a number of these patients came only once or twice. Some of them only had their histories taken and then the Willoughby done; so in a strict sense, conditioning therapy had not really begun in quite a large number of these patients. However, suppose we count all these patients, then the number of patients apparently cured or much improved is indeed about 65 percent. The comparison to make, without any question, is with the *total* number of cases treated in the psychoanalytic series (and not only with those having had more than six months' therapy). The percentage in different series thus considered varies between 31 and 42 percent. So even on this kind of comparison conditioning therapy shows up as very much the better.

I must emphasize again that the greater speed and economy of conditioning therapy are much more important than its higher percentage of recoveries. One should also remember its other merits—its experimental basis, its clearly defined methods, and the usual complete absence of unpleasant reactions during therapy.

Franks: I should like to comment briefly in reference to Dr. Stevenson's point. I think that it is a necessary and sufficient condition to know that treated patients improve, but the important thing is, when including statistics, to know if they improve more than patients who are not treated at all. The figures Dr. Stevenson gave us were 62 percent. Now, as we are aware, patients who are not treated at all seem to improve spontaneously, or for unknown reasons, at more or less the same rate—two thirds. So we have to show not merely that patients improve when they are treated, but that they improve better than untreated patients. Otherwise, why treat them? And on this basis, it is not showing anything to show that two thirds of the patients improve when treated by psychoanalytic procedures.

Gordon[1]*:* I would like to make a few remarks that will lead to some questions about the social environment of the patients involved in therapy, and about which I would like our discussants to give an

---

[1] Dr. Richard E. Gordon, Jr., Englewood, N.J.

opinion. We are all aware that many of our patients come from positions in life, and situations in life, which are very difficult for them, and for which they are very inadequately prepared. We know that older patients, divorced people, people of poor socioeconomic circumstances, people of poor intelligence, poor education, those having severe marital conflicts, or those who have difficulties with their employers, are regularly exposed to situations that realistically are dangerous to them. They are punished over and over again in their environments in the present, so that whatever suffering they endured in the past is continually being reawakened in present circumstances.

In our experience, these people not only benefit from efforts at attempting to extinguish or inhibit their abnormal responses, but they also require a great deal of teaching and learning of new skills with which to cope with these more difficult circumstances in their environment. And when something can be done to alter the environment as a result of the efforts of the therapist, their chances of recovery are greater. I should like both Mr. Salter and Dr. Wolpe to comment upon this. They touched on it slightly—Mr. Salter in his remarks, for example, about the feedback from the environment,[2] and Dr. Wolpe in his remarks on the assertive tendencies that he encourages his patients to engage in.[3] I think that these remarks are more relevant to the people who have behavior disorders, to psychopaths and psychotics, and to people with more severe reactions who are in a double-bind type of situation than they are to the mild neurotics, but I think they are relevant to all of us here, because we are also dealing with people who have not only mild disorders, but also more severe ones.

Salter: The issues raised in this question are well illustrated in the treatment of people who are in the armed forces or who work in advertising agencies. I say this because the power hierarchies there are clear and sharp. I have found that despite these power problems, and despite the patient's being low man on the totem pole, you can certainly get them to change their behavior with people who are on the same power level as they are. There is no question that certain reality situations make things extremely difficult, but a surprising number of reality situations, however, can be overcome. As for reinforcement—the individual can be taught to give himself regular and positive reinforcement and not be at the mercy of his environment —to a considerable degree.

Now people are usually, as Dr. Wolpe says, much sicker—or healthier—than they may think. I recall a woman I once treated who gave a party. After it was over she said, "I was afraid I was going to

---

[2] See page 27.
[3] See page 11.

be afraid and I was surprised when I wasn't." This ties in beautifully
with the work Dr. Lang reports (p. 45), that on a verbal level there
was one report, but on the autonomic level there was another response.

Wolpe: I agree entirely with Dr. Gordon that you have to take the social
circumstances into account, and sometimes you do find people who
are in situations in which it is—at any rate with the means at our
disposal now—impossible to overcome a neurotic state. You may find
a person who is in a chronic conflict situation—for example, being in
a terrible marriage. The circumstances arouse emotional tension, perhaps all the time. If there are also neurotic anxiety reactions they may
be relatively less important; but even if they are very important, their
treatment may be much impeded by the constant emotional disturbance due to the life circumstances. But the behavior therapist can
often instigate action leading to the resolution of difficult situations.

THE THEORY AND PRACTICE OF
CONDITIONED REFLEX THERAPY

Andrew Salter

The way out of the impasse of modern psychotherapy has nothing to do with psychoanalysis. For while the Freudian vapors of death instinct and sexual obscurantism hung in a heavy atomic cloud over much of psychiatry, in the laboratories of most of our colleges and universities a new and healthy psychology was being developed. At no time was it deceived by the transient Freudian popularity. At all times it realized one thing: broadly speaking, human emotional problems are the result of personal miseducation. It always believed that only by learning new emotional habits could the neurotic individual learn to be happy. More to the point, at all times it was insistent upon checking the truth of its findings against large groups of people, and not just talking off the cuff. In short, an objective psychology and psychiatry was being developed.

In the words of Landis (1942), "the scientific method can be applied to the problems of psychopathology—a fact known some years ago, but somehow only occasionally remembered since [the] *Interpretation of Dreams* made much of psychiatry a mad artistic speculation."

Conditioned reflex therapy is based completely on the work of Pavlov and Bechterev, and on the developments of their associates, successors, and followers. This sounds like a ritualistic statement, but I cannot help it, for it truly reflects the point of view from which I have been treating people for more than twenty years.[1]

I shall begin by discussing the theoretical basis of conditioned reflex

---

[1] This chapter explains the therapeutic methods of the author, and is not a survey of the conditioning therapies in general.

therapy. I am fully aware that translating Pavlovian concepts to human behavior may be a bit awkward at times, and occasionally, in the light of later knowledge, downright inaccurate. And I am also fully aware that with such an approach it is easy to be guilty of anthropomorphism in reverse, that is, to endow human beings with doglike characteristics. Call it Pavlomorphism. But despite these limitations, this translation—or perhaps this transfer of Pavlovian concepts—is what I have tried to do in my psychotherapeutic practice.

This is a perfectly legitimate scientific procedure, for after all, let us look at the problem. The therapist is confronted with human behavior things, just as Skinner was confronted with animal behavior things. In Gantt's (1955) very apposite words ". . . [Skinner] wishes to find out how animals behave and seeks a vocabulary that will let him talk about how they behave. Because of the existence in Sherrington and Pavlov of sets of data of the kind he believes are needed, he has adopted many of their terms and applied some of their laws in defining his area."

And that is what I have done with human beings. In Pavlov's (1927) laboratory, conditioned reflexes were originally called "psychic reflexes," and were referred to in print as "so-called psychical" activity (1928). Let us follow through Pavlov's reasoning.

Speech, of course, is the basic stimulus used in psychotherapy. In Pavlov's (1927) words, "Obviously for man speech provides conditioned stimuli which are just as real as any other stimuli. At the same time speech provides stimuli which exceed in richness and many-sidedness any of the others, allowing comparison neither qualitatively nor quantitatively with any conditioned stimuli which are possible in animals. Speech, on account of the whole preceding life of the adult, is connected up with all the internal and external stimuli which can reach the cortex, signalling all of them and replacing all of them, and therefore it can call forth all those reactions of the organism which are normally determined by the actual stimuli themselves."

In conditioned reflex therapy, speech is the stimulus. It is used by the therapist. We recognize few pregnant silences. We saturate the patient with verbal stimuli. We listen, but only to a degree.

But to what are we listening? We are listening to the private world of the patient, with all of *his* "subjective" distortions, and with all of our own. Then how can we ever be objective and quantitative with human beings, as we are with lower animals?

Laboratory objectivity, in Gantt's (1956) words, "notes and, if possible, records graphically such items as movements, secretion, heart rate, respiration, metabolism, temperature, and internal secretions in the presence of a certain stimulus in a certain environment in an individual with a certain history."

I think that by the end of this century we will be able to do precisely this with patients. Progress in electronic miniaturization will allow us to check, in our offices, how the patient "really" felt when he visited his mother last Sunday, or got up before an audience, or had an argument with his wife. At present, we have to be satisfied with the patient's distorted reports, as reinterpreted by us. Nevertheless, despite all their distortions, these reports are aspects of the patient's internal physiology. Any *qualitative* report is a *quantity of something*.

The patient can even *report* quantities:

> The *amount* of *fear*
> The *amount* of *worry*
> The *amount* of *anxiety*

and when, and where, they were elicited. And as we listen to the patient's week-by-week changes in regard to these, and other qualities, we are being objective. *More than, less than,* and *much less than* are objective relationships. A five-point scale is as much of a scale as a hundred-point scale. A diary kept by the patient is a home laboratory record.

But there is a more significant aspect to our objectivity. The concepts with which we approach the patient's material, and the concepts with which we direct the patient's activity, are all objective. Let us remember that just as Pavlov could count the number of drops of saliva secreted by a parotid gland in a dog, and flowing out of a fistula into a funnel, so can we, in psychotherapy, study the "secretions" of the human brain, coming out of the patient's mouth in the form of words.

Now this is not a matter of rhetoric or word play, this application of Pavlov to the treatment of human neuroses. I know very well that this "human verbal saliva" is much more differentiated than dog saliva—but it is also true that dog saliva varies according to the stimulus, quantitatively surely, but also even qualitatively. Pavlov observed (I am quoting Cameron, 1941) "that the type of saliva depended upon the type of food; for dry bread the secretion was copious and watery, for moist foods there was little salivation and for acids a thick saliva, designed to protect the buccal mucous membrane."

Psychological events are physiological events, and conditioning is the modification of tissue by experience. But since our knowledge of these changes is incomplete, we manufacture psychological hypotheses. The closer these hypotheses parallel physiology, the more accurate our conceptions will be, and consequently the more helpful. We do not want psychology to be a science of sterile abstractions. We are therapists—

mechanics, if you please—and the theory we want is the theory that leads us to what to do to change the material we work with. Perhaps very soon we may be able to do this chemically or electrically, but at present we do not know enough about the biochemistry and electrochemistry of the tissue modifications involved in the learning process. Surely, to tell someone that he has anxiety feelings because his cholinesterase activity is up, or because his acetylcholine production is down, will not be very helpful.

The history of the individual is stored in his protoplasm, and in his actions his history repeats itself. Through psychotherapy we manufacture new history, which repeats itself in his new actions.

Associationalism is important in understanding the origin of behavior problems, and Pavlov's differentiation between inhibition and excitation is important in understanding their treatment. Our goal is to disinhibit the inhibitory, and this we attain by what may be termed *verbal chemistry*. Words, spoken by the therapist, travel along appropriate nerve tracts in the person under treatment, and produce chemical modifications in his nervous system. These changes are associated with behavior changes, which in turn precipitate more biochemical modifications and more behavior changes.

Maladjustment is a learning process, and so is psychotherapy. Maladjustment is malconditioning, and psychotherapy is reconditioning. The individual's problems are a result of his social experiences, and by changing his techniques of social relations, we change his personality. Experience is not only the best teacher; it is the only teacher. We are not especially concerned with giving the individual stratified knowledge of his past—called "probing." What concerns us is giving him reflex knowledge for his future—called "habits."

When the individual's emotions are disinhibited, the extensive ramifications of his changed behavior prove the fundamental quality of our therapy. Consequently, to call the Pavlovian approach superficial "character analysis" as opposed to "depth analysis" is to be both inaccurate and scientifically naïve.

Although in psychotherapy we persistently emphasize excitation, certain social situations call for inhibition. Says Pavlov (1928), ". . . a continual and proper balancing of these two processes lays the basis of a normal life for both man and animal. These two opposite processes, it is necessary to add, are coexistent and equally important in the nervous activity." Gantt (Pavlov, 1928) remarks that the literal translation of Pavlov's term for disinhibition is "unbraking"—in the sense of automobile brakes—and it is this unbraking that restores the dynamic equilibrium between inhibition and excitation. In a single precept: *The solution of all problems of the self comes from unbraking the individual's behavior with other people.*

I have been particularly interested in the studies made of the physiological mechanisms underlying electric and insulin shock therapy. I think the evidence by now is overwhelmingly clear that, in Gellhorn's (1953) words, "the various procedures involved in the shock therapy of mental diseases have one significant factor in common: they involve excitation of the centers of the autonomic nervous system," and that there is "no evidence for a diminution of conditioned excitation as the result of 'shock treatment'. . . ." Some years later, Gellhorn and Loofbourrow (1963) devoted a chapter titled "Physiological Mechanisms Underlying Various Shock Therapies" (pp. 312–330) to a complete re-assessment of the problem in the light of the newer evidence. They reached essentially the same conclusions again.

Peters and Gantt (Gantt, 1958) put it well: "In all 6 courses of [electro] convulsive treatment, emotionality as reflected in general behavior was altered—the effect being determined by the temperament and the over-all emotional state of the animal prior to treatment. The change was always in the direction of less fearful, bolder 'social' responsiveness. One dog, who was chronically and pathologically fearful, approached or reached normality, depending on which treatment was used; the other dog, naturally friendly and bold, became more so; furthermore, after he had acquired a fear response, the treatments reduced or abolished it." Although electroconvulsive treatment is usually contraindicated in human neuroses, animal experimentation with it has been most helpful to the development of theory.

It certainly appears that the breaking of conditioned inhibitions is the objective of psychotherapy. The fact that anxiety is often excitatory does not affect the therapeutic objective. After all, whatever we see has to be efferent, whether it is anxiety or healthy aggression. Besides, teaching the patient other excitations eliminates the anxious excitations.

I have reported my therapeutic methods elsewhere (Salter, 1944, 1949); hence, rather than discuss them again, I shall try to explain some changes and reformulations in my techniques. These changes have evolved through a process of natural selection in my therapeutic methods. And with these changes has come a re-examination of theory, in an effort to understand the pragmatic findings.

I shall discuss these developments under four headings.

THE ORIENTING REFLEX

As a routine procedure with the majority of my cases, I have found it extremely helpful to restate their problems to them as being essentially an inhibition of the orienting reflex.

[Some recently reported Russian work, unavailable at the time this paper was originally presented, gives remarkable confirmation of this once lonely viewpoint. In the important words of E. N. Sokolov (1962), "The orienting response reflects directly the level of excitation." And conversely, "reflects directly the inhibitory relation . . ."]

In Pavlov's words (1928):

> Every sound, be it ever so small, appearing in the midst of habitual sounds and noises which surround the dog, each weakening or reinforcing of these constant sounds, each change in the intensity of the room illumination (the sun becoming hidden by the clouds, a sunbeam suddenly breaking through, a flickering of the electric lamp, a shadow across the window), the appearance of a new odour in the room, a warm or cold current of air, something touching the skin of the dog, as a fly or a falling speck of plaster from the ceiling—in all these and in endless like cases, there fatally [inexorably] begins an activity of one or another of the skeletal muscles of our animal, as of the eyelids, eyes, ears, nostrils; or the head or the trunk or some other part of the body will turn and take a new position; and these movements are either repeated and reinforced, or the animal becomes fixed in a certain pose.
>
> We have before us again a special reaction of the organism, a reflex of the simple kind which we call an *orienting* or *focusing* reflex. If in the surroundings of the animal there appears some new agent (by this I include changes in the intensity of previously acting agents), then the corresponding receptor surfaces of the organism become focused on it, in a manner which will bring about the most favorable stimulation.

Somehow, I have found this concept of inhibition of the orienting reflex to have a very strong impact on the patient. I speak as follows, and oversimplify the theory:

"Wouldn't that be a pretty sad dog," I say, "if he entered a new place, and didn't paw around, sniff, prick his ears, and respond externally? Well, we have more complex nervous systems than the dog—but let's learn from him as a start."

I previously called my technique of freeing the orienting reflex "feeling talk," that is, the deliberate utterance of spontaneously felt emotions. If the patient likes the soup, he is to say, out loud, "I like the soup." He is to put his emotional responses into his verbomotor system.

"That shade of green is perfect for you." This externalization of praise, *if it is honestly felt,* is more feeling talk. I have elsewhere listed such feelings—among others—as like, dislike, praise, relief, complaint, determination, impatience, discomfort, enjoyment, appreciation, curiosity, and skepticism (Salter, 1949).

Somehow, nevertheless, recasting the externalization of affect as "*disinhibiting the inhibited orienting reflex*" reaches many patients quickly.

A young man recently told a young lady that he was consulting me. "Oh," she said, when he mentioned my name. "Isn't that the fellow who has you get into fights in restaurants?" Sometimes. But we also praise the food, when the food merits praise.

My writings on the importance of externalizing aggression have received a great deal of comment. I do not withdraw one word of them, but aggression, nevertheless, is only one of the many verbomotor possibilities. It is an important motor possibility, but it is only one of many others.

What of the anxious, hyper-reactive patient? Isn't this the orienting reflex gone wild? Isn't this excitation with very little cortical inhibition? It is indeed.

This is what we see in the low–self-sufficiencied obsessive talker. Nevertheless, there is one important difference between this and healthy excitation: there is no *feedback* from the environment. The patient is not responding to the *fluctuations* of his environment, but is simply pouring out increasingly unrelated responses, with few adjustive reactions to the variations in his immediate environment. In the treatment of such patients it is futile to tell them to inhibit. But to point out to them that they are not *responding* to the specific *fluctuations* in the environment turns out to be much more effective therapeutically.

AUTOKINESIS AND SCHIZOKINESIS

The second development that I have made in my therapeutic techniques is to recast some of my thinking around Gantt's (1953a, 1953b, 1956, 1958) concepts of autokinesis and schizokinesis. To quote,

> *Autokinesis* is the term for the ability of the organism to develop, to acquire new responses on the basis of old stimulations and their traces, and to change its relationships to the old stimulations without the aid of any new external stimulation. Sometimes it is the antithesis of schizokinesis. Autokinesis is a dynamic quality, a progressing elaboration rather than a static mechanism. It can have both a therapeutic as well as a pathological implication (Gantt, 1953b).

I have found the concept of autokinesis helpful in explaining the profound and sustained results in relatively brief therapy. I find here also the explanation of the chapter, in my *Conditioned Reflex Therapy,* titled "The Constructive Use of Past Conditionings." In Gantt's (1956) words, "A future physiology, embracing autokinetic functions—the laws of development and interaction among the traces of past experiences— may reveal even more than the study of our relations to the external environment."

"Negative autokinesis" (Gantt, 1958) explains the elaboration of the varied masochistic and self-defeating patterns of the patient in the absence of any significant additional environmental conditioning. Every therapist has seen this operate.

I have found that it is usually possible to mobilize, and set working, the "positive autokinesis" latent in the majority of office patients—call it the "reflexological will to health."

The concept of schizokinesis gives the answer to those patients of mine (the vast majority) who ask me, "Why do I have to say it out loud? Can't I just think it?" I answer this by saying, "All of your life, by inhibiting your emotional impulses, you have created your present problems. You will continue this neurotic pattern until you *do* say it out loud and thus disinhibit your responses. Feeling it is only half of it. Saying it, getting it into your muscles is the other half." More generally (Dykman, Gantt, Whitehorn, 1956), ". . . we believe that normal healthy learning is characterized by an *integration* of autonomic and motor responses, at both the emotional and problem-solving levels. It is suggested that any lack of integration (schizokinesis) occurring at any point in the conditioning process is indicative of psychopathology."

In my opinion, the aim of conditioned reflex therapy is the repair of this cleavage, the removal of this schizokinesis, by the rewelding of the autonomic and motor systems. In union is strength and mental health.

In the quotation from Dykman, Gantt, and Whitehorn cited immediately above, it will be noted that they point out that healthy learning has integration of autonomic and motor responses on *both* the emotional and problem-solving levels. I consider this finding to provide an important theoretical basis for my earlier observation: "Feeling-talk of the 'I like the soup' and 'I don't like the meat' variety, is always indicated, but most important is vigorous excitation directed toward the solution of problems of interpersonal relations" (Salter, 1949). Also, in this connection, I have emphasized the importance of "conditions which give the animal *increased mastery of its environment*" and the fact that "On the human level it is excitation that means environmental mastery" (Salter, 1949). I mention my interest in "problem-solving" because years ago I found that although I could condition away distress about unsolved problems, greater therapeutic progress came from actually solving the problems.

THE QUANTITATIVE APPROACH TO
INHIBITION AND EXCITATION

I should like now to turn to my third point. In my practice I have become increasingly interested in a quantitative approach to inhibition and excitation.

Certain laboratory stimuli reduce the secretion of saliva more than others. And certain interpersonal situations cause more inhibition than others. When I wrote about this some years ago I said that with some persons it was best to begin therapy with their work relationships, and that with others it was sometimes best to start with their home relationships.

Implicit in this was the idea that it is best to start disinhibition and problem-solving where the level of inhibition is lowest. I always pressed where the leverage was maximal, that is, where minimum effort could produce the most immediate disinhibitory rewards. This automatic reinforcement of affect, and the diminution of the inhibitory level, then made what I called "heavier inhibitory weights" easier to lift.

I still seek the easier levels of disinhibition, but I do it more deliberately now, and find that as treatment progresses the higher levels of inhibition constantly get lower.

In this connection, the classical Pavlovian explanation of neurosis as the result of a conflict between inhibition and excitation wears very well in the treatment of human neurosis. In practice, seeking what has been inhibited, and helping it to become motor—within social and legal limits —makes therapy move at a fast pace indeed.

Gantt (1953b) has pointed out that "this expression of our behavior in the simple terms 'excitation' and 'inhibition' is too schematic to describe completely so complex a phenomenon. But there are many advantages. . . ."

I have made my definitions of inhibition and excitation on the human level, and, if we accept Pavlov's concept of the second signaling system, my definitions are valid. I grant that we can use a great deal more knowledge about excitation and inhibition, but I want to suggest that we need not be self-conscious about what we do know now, and what we can apply in psychotherapy.

Gasser has given us an excellent definition of "inhibition" (Florey, 1961), and when it comes to human psychotherapy it will suffice:

[Inhibition] is a term of convenience used without exact definition in connection with a group of phenomena having certain qualities in common. The essential condition is the stoppage or prevention of action through the temporary operation of a process which does not harm the tissue. It is usually also implied that the process results from nervous activity, or imitates the result of nervous activity.

Although we solemnly allege that the theories we work with are experimentally supported and internally consistent, and that our therapeutic practices are derived solely from these theories, the fact remains that our therapeutic techniques and our results can be evaluated quite apart from these theoretical bases.

LURIA AND THE ROLE OF SPEECH

The last point which I shall consider is the meaning for psychotherapy of Luria's recently published researches. I have found that they provide a sound theoretical basis for certain effective therapeutic techniques, whose theory had previously been somewhat weak; and I also think that they suggest some new therapeutic emphases.

We may discuss Luria's findings without being disturbed by Masserman's criticism of the experimental procedure. Masserman (1951) was distressed at "the possibility that requiring either male or female subjects to squeeze a rubber bulb (the Luria technique) may have introduced erotically symbolic distortions."

The title of Luria's book (1961) states the area of his experimentation: *The Role of Speech in the Regulation of Normal and Abnormal Behavior.* Luria is concerned with the development and permeation of *speech in the brain:* Pavlov's second signaling system.

The development of speech begins with the mother acting as her child's verbal conditioner. She points to an object and names it. The word, says Luria, begins to serve "a complex task of analysis and synthesis for the child, and later settles into a complex system of links acting on him and conditioning his behavior."

A little later the child reaches a stage where he can point to the objects named by his mother, and can even name them himself. Now, says Luria, the child has become "capable of *actively modifying the environment that influences him;* by using speech for himself, he alters the relative strength of the stimuli acting upon him, and *adapts his behavior to the influences thus modified.*"

But the welding of speech to action is still not complete. Says Luria, "Try, for example, giving a child of twenty months to two years verbal instructions to take its stockings *off* while it is pulling them *on* . . . or to put rings *on* a bar while it is taking them *off,* and you will see that your verbal instructions are unable to alter the action already begun; on the contrary, they will merely intensify it. Thus at this stage of development the child's action still predominates: although the adult's speech has already assumed an initiating function, it cannot yet inhibit an action once started, much less *switch the child from one action to another.*"

Nevertheless, says Luria, "Does this mean that it is quite impossible to get a young child to perform a voluntary action consisting of the inhibition of a motor action already begun and the subordination of movement to inhibitory verbal impulses? The fact that at this age the direct inhibitory function of speech is not yet developed, and that adult speech which attempts to inhibit nonvolitional motor reactions often operates unspecifically and only intensifies the motor reaction, does not prevent us from seeking the beginnings of the organization of volitional movement."

Through ingenious but relatively simple experimentation, Luria traces the development of what I will term *heteroregulation* of the child's activity through adult speech, and the acquisition by the child of what I will term *autoregulation* and internal speech.

Luria demonstrates, in the most convincing detail, that "the speech system, which is formed in the process of the child's social intercourse with the adult, is a powerful means of systematic organization of our mental processes. . . ."

Luria's work proves that the second signaling system of words and language is even more important than we had ever suspected before. The Pavlov-Bechterev explanation of hypnosis, which I enlarged upon in an earlier publication (Salter, 1944), and which some critics considered to be an unfair extension of the hitherto reported work in conditioning, must now, on the strength of Luria's experimentation, be considered completely valid.

Luria's work also sheds light on autokinesis and schizokinesis in humans. With verbal patterns so fully permeating the cortex, and with the contents of the cortex in a large sense even built around these verbal patterns, the slightest self-stimulation of these cerebral traces can conduce to auto-elaboration toward health, or toward sickness.

Luria also gives us the explanation for the widely reported finding that optimism and mental health conduce toward hypnotizability. Why should it be otherwise? The individual whose verbal and motor systems have been well soldered to each other is an individual who, on average, in his growing-up period accepted the verbal-motor conditioning of his environment. Verbal stimulation, autosuggested or heterosuggested, will elicit his responses.

But what of the individual whose early years were filled with contradiction and conflict? The result is inevitable. To such persons a word becomes a *thing-that-you-do-the-opposite-of.*

We see it clearly with older children. Words will take no hold when an adult states one meaning and then completely reverses it. For instance, a parent says, "I love you so much, Charlie," and, in the next breath says, "Why can't you be more like Johnny?"

How *can* words acquire standard meanings when they keep contradicting themselves? Take this, for instance:

"Mother, may I have some ice cream now?"

"No. You may not have any ice cream before dinner."

An argument ensues.

"All right," says the mother. "Just this once."

Is it any wonder that a verbal-motor schism develops? Words from the external environment become conditioned to mean *things-you-do-not-do.* The environment is a chronic enemy. *Words-from-others* are never *words-for-me.* Here is the explanation for what I shall call the *primary negativity* of most neurotics. Verbal stimuli from the outside can't really get into the patient's nervous system. The patients (and every therapist sees many of them) become "aginners," subtle or obvious, but "aginners" nevertheless. How is it possible to treat such persons, or must we reject them for therapy?

In treating such persons the natural tendency is to try to hack away at the insulation that separates their verbal system from their motor system. But to hack away at "aginners" is to mobilize more of their negativism, although there are some exceptions. We get the solution to the dilemma by approaching this as a matter of pure conditioning. In a sense, there is really no insulation between the "aginners' " verbal and motor systems. When you say, "Stand up" to them, in their personally conditioned language you are really saying, "*Don't* stand up." When you say to them, "*Don't* stand up," you are really saying, "*Stand* up." It's like having a dog and naming him Pussy-cat. Before long, whenever you say, "Here, Pussy-cat," your dog will come running to you.

What I do with these "aginners" is to try to recondition their verbal systems all at once. "Pavlov," I explain, "spoke of a reflex of freedom and a reflex of slavery. Now," I continue, "you call what you are doing *freedom.* I doubt that it is true freedom, but let it pass. However, what I want to do with you is to restore your reflex of slavery, to a point. Yes, reflex of slavery. I want to make you a slave again."

This horrifies them, of course. I then explain their self-defeating negativistic conditioning from Luria's viewpoint, and as I explain how to become a slave—how to let the environment dominate, how to surrender— as I explain this with concrete illustrations from their personal life, more often than not we make substantial progress in a half-dozen sessions, after the first few preliminary ones.

I shall close with two quotations. One is from Freud and one is from Pavlov.

Said Freud (1948), "These circuitous ways to death . . . would be neither more nor less than the phenomena of life as we now know it . . . the whole life of instinct serves the one end of bringing about death."

Pavlov (1928) said the exact opposite: "All life is nothing other than the realisation of one purpose, *viz.*, the preservation of life itself, the tireless labour of which may be called the general *instinct of life.*"

The theories and the therapies stemming from these completely opposite viewpoints will be resolved in this century. At this time one thing is clear. Psychoanalysis is at last on the defensive.

REFERENCES

CAMERON, D. E. *Objective and experimental psychiatry.* New York: Macmillan, 1941.

DYKMAN, R. A., GANTT, W. H., & WHITEHORN, J. C. Conditioning as emotional sensitization and differentiation. *Psychol. Monogr.,* 1956, *70,* 17.

FLOREY, E. (Ed.) *Nervous inhibition.* New York: Pergamon, 1961.

FREUD, S. *Beyond the pleasure principle.* London: Hogarth, 1948. (1st ed., German, 1920.)

GANTT, W. H. Principles of nervous breakdown—schizokinesis and autokinesis. *Ann. N.Y. Acad. Sci.,* 1953, *56,* 143–163 (a).

GANTT, W. H. The physiological basis of psychiatry: The conditional reflex. In J. Wortis (Ed.), *Basic problems in psychiatry.* New York: Grune & Stratton, 1953 (b).

GANTT, W. H. Book review of Estes, W. K., Koch, S., MacCorquodale, K., Meehl, P. E., Mueller, C. G., Schoenfeld, W. N., & Verplanck, W. S. *Modern learning theory.* In *Hum. Biol.,* 1955, *27,* 50.

GANTT, W. H. *Medicine in a changing society.* New York: International Universities, 1956.

GANTT, W. H. (Ed.) *Physiological bases of psychiatry.* Springfield, Ill.: Charles C Thomas, 1958.

GELLHORN, E. *Physiological foundations of neurology and psychiatry.* Minneapolis: U. Minnesota Press, 1953.

GELLHORN, E., & LOOFBOURROW, G. N. *Emotions and emotional disorders.* New York: Harper, 1963.

LANDIS, C. Book review of D. E. Cameron, *Objective and experimental psychiatry* (ed. 2). *J. abnorm. soc. Psychol.,* 1942, *37,* 141–142.

LURIA, A. R. *The role of speech in the regulation of normal and abnormal behavior.* New York: Liveright, 1961.

MASSERMAN, J. Discussion. *Amer. J. Psychiat.*, 1951, *108,* 287.

PAVLOV, I. P. *Conditioned reflexes.* London: Oxford U. Press, 1927.

PAVLOV, I. P. *Lectures on conditioned reflexes.* New York: International Publishers (W. H. Gantt, Ed.), 1928.

SALTER, A. *What is hypnosis?* New York: Richard R. Smith, 1944; Farrar, Straus, 1955; Citadel, 1963.

SALTER, A. *Conditioned reflex therapy.* New York: Farrar, Straus, 1949; Capricorn Books-Putnam's Sons, 1961.

SOKOLOV, E. N. In R. A. Bauer (Ed.) *Some views on Soviet psychology.* Washington, D.C.: American Psychological Association, 1962.

DISCUSSION

Stevenson: In the first place, in regard to the importance of antecedent experiences in the etiology of neuroses, the Pavlovians are, to put it briefly, "Johnny-come-latelies." Pavlov himself, certainly in all of his early work, emphasized the recent task, and I think he paid little or no attention to the different types of animals (which might include their antecedent experiences) until the Leningrad flood drew his attention to the different kinds of responses of the animals to that stress. Although it is perfectly true, as Dr. Bailey says[1], that Freud and the analysts did not discover the importance of early experiences, they did, I think, emphasize the importance of these experiences, which is a considerable contribution.

Much of the language of psychoanalysis uses expressions employed by Mr. Salter. Freud wrote a paper, for example, on psychotherapy as re-education. Over and over again, he talks about a neurosis as exposing the history of the patient. The expression "schism," for example, seems to me to be a somewhat different word for the psychoanalytic concept of dissociation. I think it's terribly important that we not be swindled into believing that something new has come when only our vocabulary has been changed, or to modify the analogy, that we not be sold old wine in new bottles.

I hasten to add that I myself am thoroughly convinced that the behaviorists are fermenting new wine, but I do wish that we could sharpen up some of the issues in which the psychoanalysts and the behaviorists can really be discriminated, and I would like to mention just two of these issues. One of them is this: Is a particular experience occurring in the first five years of life more important in the etiology of neurosis than a similar experience occurring, say, in the fourth five years of life? This is something that the analysts have mentioned for sixty years. I think that the evidence, on the whole,

---

[1] See page 95.

supports their position, and certainly the recent evidence in studies of maternal deprivation.

Now take the second point on which we might discriminate issues. What is the relevance of repression in the etiology of neuroses and of derepression in the recovery? The analysts have contended that derepression—I say that they *have* contended, because I don't think that this is quite true now, though it is still a part of psychoanalytic theory—the analysts have contended that derepression is a requirement for full recovery from a neurosis. Now that seems to be, on the evidence that Dr. Wolpe and others, including myself, have presented, clearly false. You can get over a psychoneurosis without having your early experiences derepressed. But if you go further and you say, "Is derepression ever helpful? Is it therapeutic?" you might be tempted to say, "No, it's not," and that would be quite incorrect. You would be wrong again, because there is evidence that derepression is helpful to certain patients.

Well, these are just illustrations of the importance, as I see it, of trying to get at particular issues, in which these two groups of people might uphold different points on narrowly defined issues.

Salter: I must say that I find the praise of Freud as a great educator somewhat confusing. The names that come to my mind, as being associated with the development of concepts of education and learning, are those of Thorndike, Lashley, Watson, and Pavlov. All of Freud's writings pay absolutely no attention to any of the extensive scientific work on learning.

Dollard and Miller (1950) were fully aware of this deficiency, and attempted to translate the analytic version of psychotherapy into learning terms. In this spirit, they dedicated their book to "Freud and Pavlov and their students." But since their index listed forty-five references to Freud, and only eight references to Pavlov, their dedication must be labeled as erroneous and misleading, and so also, I think, are all other efforts to bring Freud into the camp of "scientific psychology and psychiatry."

I think the question of early experience calls for some comment. Dr. Stevenson is quite right. "Freud and the analysts did not discover the importance of early experiences," but I cannot agree with him in praising the analysts for emphasizing the importance of early experiences. The question is, *what* early experiences?

Now, Freud said so many things in so many different ways that, if you look at his last book, *An Outline of Psychoanalysis* (1949), where he included all his revisions and modifications, you will find out that he still believed that the *only,* I repeat *only,* early experiences of any significance in the manufacture of neurosis were the sexual experiences. Those were the early experiences that concerned Freud to his dying day. The addition of the theory of the "death instinct" did not alter Freud's basic concern. In his last book he says that "we come upon an interesting discrepancy between theory and experience. Theoretically there is no objection to supposing that any sort of instinctual demand whatever could occasion these same repressions and their consequences; but our observation shows us invariably, so far as we can judge, that the excitations that play this pathogenic part arise from the component instincts of sexual life. The symptoms of neuroses are exclusively, it might be said, either a substitutive satisfaction of some sexual impulse or measures to prevent such a satisfaction, and are as a rule compromises between the two. . . ."

I am happy to see that Freud's emphasis upon the unconscious has not been cited as a great contribution, for Freud did not emphasize the unconscious. Freud emphasized the *sexual* unconscious, which is an entirely different matter. Freud himself, interestingly enough, never took credit for this contemporary analytic rewriting of history. Freud made it very clear in the last page he ever wrote (1950): "The concept of the unconscious has long been knocking at the gates of psychology and asking to be let in. Philosophy and literature have often toyed with it, but science could find no use for it. Psycho-analysis has seized upon the concept, has taken it seriously and has given it a fresh content."

Whyte's well-documented book, *The Unconscious before Freud* (1960), I think, is complete and devastating in establishing that the unconscious had a long and honorable history before Freud.

All of us, analysts included, are trying to describe what we see among people, so all of us will have certain points of contact. But Freud's contribution sinks or swims on the complete sexualization of all human impulses, so similarities of Pavlovian theory to Freudian theory are of no fundamental significance.

Wolpe: Dr. Stevenson said that he feels that derepression, though not necessary, is sometimes helpful. I think even that is extremely doubtful. It is true that sometimes in the bringing forth of memories and the recounting of past experiences, there is an emotional arousal after which the patient may be better. This may happen in one interview or there may be several emotional arousals over several interviews, after which the patient is better; but one cannot say that it is because of the emergence of the memories that this happens. What leads to recovery may be the emotional arousal due to the recounting of the experience. Grinker and Spiegel's (1943, 1945) work on war neuroses showed that it did not really matter whether the emotionally evocative material was remembered by the patient or not at the time when he brought it forth.

Question: Would Mr. Salter illustrate how, or with what examples, he exhorts patients to slavery?

Salter: That has a frightening sound. It is not a question of simply saying, "I am now going to exhort you into slavery." First, it is important to go over the whole viewpoint that the individual had, while growing up, about refusing to be a slave to his environment. With a husband who constantly fights being "henpecked," the formulation to him would be that slavery *consists* of being henpecked. I don't want to say that just restating the individual's problems as a matter of restoring slavery results in instant cure. I simply want to say that as the concept is developed over a session or two, and is then applied in regard to the patient's wife, in regard to his children (he will usually refuse to give in to the demands of his children), in regard to his co-workers (So-and-so is always asking him to do things, and he refuses to do these things, and disguises his refusal), as you develop the concept of slavery with concrete illustrations, the reformulation has a strong and rapid therapeutic effect.

REFERENCES

DOLLARD, J., & MILLER, N. E. *Personality and psychotherapy: An analysis in terms of learning, thinking and culture.* New York: McGraw-Hill, 1950.

FREUD, S. *An outline of psychoanalysis.* (Originally published 1940) New York: Norton, 1949.

FREUD, S. *Collected papers.* Vol. V. (Paper originally published 1941) London: Hogarth, 1950.

GRINKER, R. R., & SPIEGEL, J. P. *War neurosis in North Africa.* New York: Macy, 1943.

GRINKER, R. R., & SPIEGEL, J. P. *Men under stress.* New York: Blakiston, 1945.

WHYTE, L. L. *The unconscious before Freud.* New York: Basic, 1960.

EXPERIMENTAL STUDIES OF
DESENSITIZATION PSYCHOTHERAPY

Peter J. Lang, Ph.D.

I would like to discuss a program of research that is being carried on by Dr. A. David Lazovik and myself at the University of Pittsburgh.[1] I propose to talk about the data that we have been gathering, speculate about them, and suggest the direction which I anticipate future research will take. Specifically, this project is concerned with the experimental investigation of behavior therapy. Currently we are focusing on systematic desensitization therapy (Wolpe, 1958).

Desensitization therapy is designed for the treatment of anxiety and phobic reactions. It represents a direct attempt at substituting muscular re-laxation responses for the tension response of anxiety. An early experiment of Mary Cover Jones (1924) provided the original model for this tech-nique. You may recall that she was able to countercondition a young boy's fear of small animals. Her method involved gradual exposure to the feared object. As a first step, a caged rabbit was introduced into the therapy room. It was placed at a considerable distance from the child, who was sitting in a high chair and eating a favorite food. Over a series of sessions, the rabbit was moved closer and closer to the subject. At each stage the child was fed, sometimes in the company of unafraid peers or friendly adults. Eventually, he sat happily with the rabbit upon his lap. At the termination of therapy he also showed little or no fear when exposed to other small animals, and a generally increased tolerance for unfamiliar situations.

---

[1] This research project is supported by NIMH Grant M-3880. Dr. Lang is now at the University of Wisconsin.

Jones attributed these results to the gradual replacement of fear by the positive responses (alimentary and social) associated with feeding. This method of "successive approximations" of the stimulus appears to be extremely effective. Meyer (1957) employed an analogous technique in the treatment of actual clinical cases. Hospital patients, afraid of open or closed places, overcame their fears when, according to a planned regimen, the therapist slowly introduced them to these stimuli. More recently, this approach has been effective in the treatment of children with school phobias (Klein, 1961).

There are, however, obvious problems in applying this method along the complete spectrum of anxiety neuroses. The main difficulty is the inconvenience, and in many cases the impossibility, of facing individual patients with the actual objects of their fear. One cannot readily bring unique social situations, anxiety about specific authority figures or sexual relationships, into the therapist's office. And unless the patient is in a hospital, it is not usually possible for the therapist to accompany the patient and actively measure out his exposure to life stresses. Wolpe has overcome this problem very nicely in his desensitization method: the stimuli are presented as visualized scenes.

The first step in desensitization therapy is to have the individual define the feared object or events. He is then helped to develop an "anxiety hierarchy." This is a series of situations or events related to the object of fear, which are ranked in order of fearfulness. Thus, items high in the hierarchy are very frightening, and central to the phobia; the other items are progressively more remote from the main stimulus for anxiety. Instead of presenting, as Mary Cover Jones did, the actual phobic object, scenes involving the fear stimuli are presented as hypnotically experienced events. At first, instead of being far away spatially, the individual is far away in terms of *psychological proximity* to the phobic object.

The response used to countercondition fear is not a positive alimentary response, but deep muscle relaxation (Jacobson, 1938). The central hypothesis is that you cannot be both relaxed and anxious simultaneously. These two responses are incompatible or reciprocally inhibit each other. If the subject can be trained to make a response to the phobic object which is incompatible with fear or anxiety, the phobia is eliminated. There are many clinical reports of success with this method (Rachman, 1959; Wolpe, 1958, 1961). My own observations of patients treated in this manner have generally been consistent with these findings.

The present investigation was designed to examine desensitization therapy in a laboratory setting. We wanted to evaluate this method under conditions of rigorous experimental control. This consideration seemed to eliminate the use of a patient population as subjects. The demands of a research design could easily be compromised by the necessary, special consideration of individual patients. But on the other hand, can you find people who are not clinic cases and who would nevertheless show phobias or anxiety reactions? In an effort to deal with this impasse, we distributed a questionnaire to freshman psychology students, asking them to report their fears. They were specifically asked to list only those fears which did not involve the real possibility of danger or pain. The students turned out to be quite cooperative, and the questionnaires have considerable intrinsic interest.

An "irrational" fear that appeared very frequently, and the one with which we have done the most work so far, concerned nonpoisonous snakes. Such a fear does not interfere greatly with one's adjustment to city life. A person does not have to worry about coming upon snakes, except perhaps on vacation trips or in the park. Nevertheless, a number of students (one or two per hundred questioned) have very intense fears of harmless snakes, and this fear frequently shows wide generalization. For example, one subject reported that his mother would remove photographs of snakes from magazines, before he read them, because of his fear and distress at seeing such pictures. It was students of this type—those with severe phobic reactions—whom we tried to enlist in our project. However, it is important to note that these were people who would ordinarily not seek help. With the exception of a petroleum engineering student, who was concerned that his fear of snakes might interfere with his career, the phobias worked with here were not significant life problems for our subjects. This fact permitted us to be more systematic in our application of the therapy than would have been possible had actual patients been used.

The experimental therapy was worked out by Dr. Lazovik and myself and tested on a pilot sample of four subjects (1960). Three of these individuals showed a significant reduction in fear following treatment. This result encouraged us to begin an extensive investigation of this technique.

The laboratory analogue of desensitization therapy paralleled the clinical process in every way, except for the experimental requirement of rigorous method. The therapist was cued, in each session, by a mimeographed program of procedure. A great majority of the communications to the subject were actually read from prepared sheets. I do not mean to imply that the subject and the therapist did not develop a relationship. The therapist was not unfriendly. He did not go out of his way to be a negative stimulus. However, an attempt was made to standardize the contacts as much as possible. Furthermore, the subjects were told that the experimenter did not necessarily expect success. His attitude was that of a scientist. He was more interested in a factual evaluation than in positive results.

The procedure divided into two main units, training and desensitization. During the five training sessions a twenty-item "anxiety hierarchy" was developed, and the subjects were trained in muscle relaxation and hypnosis. Subsequently, each subject experienced eleven desensitization sessions. The "anxiety hierarchies" were, of course, individually created with each subject. An example of a minimally fear-evoking scene would be, "sitting with a notebook on the lap and writing down the word 'snake.' " A subsequent item might involve seeing an outline drawing of a snake. A moving picture of a live, active snake would be more frightening. Further along in the hierarchy the subject might be asked to imagine he was present when a naturalist transferred a snake from one cage to another. Final items involved the visualization of actual contact with a live, tame snake. At the beginning of each desensitization session, subjects were instructed to relax deeply. They then visualized each scene for a standard period of time. Scenes which elicited anxiety were repeated until the subject reported they no longer interrupted his calm state. At this point the next successive item was broached, and this process was continued for all eleven therapy sessions.

The most difficult problem in the experimental study of psychotherapy concerns measurement. In the present research we are interested in developing methods of reducing fear behavior. But what is fear, when it is considered as the dependent variable in an experiment? Our analysis of this question led to the conclusion that the concept of fear (or anxiety) is associated with three measurable behaviors: verbal, motor, and somatic. The verbal aspect of fear is clearly illustrated by the patient's statement, "I am afraid." It is also revealed in disturbances of speech pattern or verbal recall. The main motor component is simple avoidance. The individual who is afraid of heights requests a hotel room on the first floor. A hooded rat, shocked previously in the black compartment, jumps a barrier into the white enclosure. The motor component may also show itself in failures of coordination or "displacement behavior." The third relevant sector of behavior involves the muscular and autonomic substrate of fear. Distress is betrayed by alterations in respiration, cardiac rate, and blood pressure, and by a decrease in skin resistance and an increase in electromyographic levels.

No one of these behaviors is fear. A particular sector may give out a false lead. Thus, an individual may say he is unafraid, while his manifest avoidance behavior and heightened somatic activity send a different message. On the other hand, disturbances in somatic activity may be a function of emotional states other than fear or organic disease. Even avoidance behavior does not constitute a completely reliable estimate of fear, if no account is taken of the other activity just described. Ideally, all three sectors of behavior should be evaluated. In the research I will describe now, verbal and overt avoidance indicants of fear were measured. I will describe the beginnings of our work with somatic measurement later on.

The motor response used in this study involved actual avoidance of the phobic object. Following an interview, the subject is asked if he will come to a nearby laboratory, observe a harmless snake, and describe his feelings. If he agrees, the subject and the experimenter together enter a room that is roughly fifteen feet across. There is a glass aquarium at the opposite end, and in this aquarium is a tame, five-foot pilot black snake (*Elaphe obsoleta obsoleta*). The subject remains at the door. The experimenter walks over to the glass case and lifts off the wire cover. While he stands and observes the snake, he invites the subject to approach. Generally, phobic subjects will not approach the animal with the first request. If the subject remains at the door, he is invited to come as close as he is able. His distance in feet from the phobic object is recorded. This constitutes a simple runway test of avoidance, analogous to a method commonly used in animal research. If, on the other hand, the subject walks to a point immediately in front of the snake, the experimenter—quite casually—touches the snake and invites the subject to do this. If he refuses, that is the end of the test. If the subject touches the snake, the experimenter reaches into the aquarium and picks it up. He then invites the subject to hold the snake. The test is ended following the subject's refusal, or acquiescence. Each request is made twice. Following the test, the subject's behavior—touching, holding, or his distance in feet from the snake—is noted. The experimenter also rates the subject on overt signs of anxiety.

The primary measure used to evaluate verbal fear behavior was first used in a study of parachutists (Walk, 1956). They were asked to note their fear before and after jumps. In the present experiment, the subject is asked to rate his anxiety immediately following exposure to the snake avoidance test. He circles a number on a ten-point rating scale. After the number "1" is written, "completely relaxed." The number "10" is followed by the words, "scared as I've ever been." Prior to treatment, phobic subjects generally circled "8," "9," and, occasionally, "10." We called this scale the "fear thermometer."

The Fear Survey Schedule (FSS) provided a second measure of verbal behavior. This instrument was a list of fifty fears or phobias, each followed by a seven-point scale, extending from "no fear" to "terror." This was used to provide a measure of generalization. We were interested in discovering if a change in the snake fear would affect the incidence or intensity of other fears.

In addition to the formal measures, we conducted extensive taped interviews before and after therapy. Subjects were questioned about their motivation for change, and their reasons for volunteering for the project. We explored a number of areas of living, with an eye on the issue of symptom substitution.

Symptom substitution was actually one of the main questions we wished to investigate in this experiment. If we were successful in eliminating a phobia, would some other fear take its place? We were also interested in evaluating the role of relaxation, hypnosis, and rapport. To what extent are they responsible for the changes effected by desensitization therapy?

The plan of the experiment (Lang, 1963) included two experimental groups, both of which experienced desensitization therapy, and two control groups. Control subjects did not participate in therapy, but were evaluated (avoidance test, interview, and "fear thermometer") at the same times as the experimental subjects. Experimental (E-1) and control (C-1) groups were evaluated before training (Test 1), after training (Test 2) and following desensitization (Test 3). The E-2 and C-2 groups did not receive the pretraining testing, but participated in the other two evaluation sessions. This design allowed for the separate estimation of effects attributable to the training period—effects associated with the suggestion to change implicit in participating in the experiment, being hypnotized, and learning muscular relaxation. All subjects were also evaluated six months after the experimental group completed therapy. They are currently being seen at one-year posttherapy follow-up sessions.

The avoidance test findings for thirteen experimental subjects and eleven controls are presented in Table 1. It was difficult to decide how to present these data. Simple arithmetic differences scores (pre-test minus post-test) are not appropriate. It seems that the avoidance gradient grows steeper as the subject moves closer to the phobic object. A change from three feet away to two feet away from the phobic object seems to rep-

TABLE 1
Number of Subjects Who Held or Touched the Snake during the Avoidance Test

Group	N	Test 1	Test 2	Test 3
E–1	8	1	1	5
E–2	5	—	1	2
C–1	5	0	0	0
C–2	6	—	1	2
E–1 & E–2	13		2	7
C–1 & C–2	11		1	2

resent greater improvement than a movement from twelve to eleven feet. Before trying to develop a continuous measure which would consider this problem, we evaluated changes in terms of a simple dichotomy. The criterion was: Does the subject touch or hold the animal during the avoidance test? As can be seen in Table 1, this evaluation indicated considerable change from Test 2 to Test 3 in our experimental group, and relatively little in the control group. On the other hand, no change is associated with training (Test 1 to Test 2).

It will be noticed that even at Test 1, a phobic subject was willing to touch the snake. This is interesting, because all these people, in terms of verbal behavior, were extremely frightened. But, as I previously suggested, the separate sectors of behavior do not always correlate. There are also some data that the disparity is greater in psychotics. Dr. R. D. Cowden, of the Leech Farm Veterans Administration Hospital, administered our evaluation procedure to schizophrenic subjects who were snake phobic (Cowden, Reynolds, and Ford, 1961). Little relationship was found between verbal reports of fear and avoidance test behavior. The interaction between verbal, overt, and somatic behavior systems deserves increased study.

Our attempts to develop a continuous measure of change in avoidance test behavior led to a ratio measure. First we assigned subjects a performance score. This was defined by a scale beginning with 1 (holding the snake), 2 (touching), and with successive numbers assigned for each foot away from the test animal. To obtain the subject's final score, his scale score at Test 3 was subtracted from his Test 2 score, and then divided by the Test 2 score. The results using this subtler measure are presented in Table 2. The mean change score from Test 2 to Test 3 is greater for the experimental subjects than for controls. This difference is statistically significant.

TABLE 2

Mean Snake Avoidance Scale Score at Test 2 and 3, Mean Change Scores, and the Mann-Whitney Test of Significance

	Test 2	Test 3	Change scores	U
Experimental groups	5.35	4.42	0.34	
Control groups	6.51	7.73	−0.19	34.5[a]

[a] $p < .05$

Our estimates of verbal behavior also suggested differences between groups. Mean reduction in fear, as estimated by the "fear thermometer," was greater for experimental subjects than for controls. However, this difference was not statistically significant. Nevertheless, at the six-month follow-up investigation the verbal behavior caught up. The subjects not only behaved less fearfully in terms of overt avoidance, but reported significantly less anxiety on both the "fear thermometer" and the snake item of the Fear Survey Schedule. This is especially interesting because most traditional therapists attempt to alter verbal behavior, hoping that the effects will generalize to overt behavior. As we know, this has not proved to be very successful. The present method seems directly to change overt behavior, which subsequently spreads to verbal behavior. It will be interesting to observe concurrent autonomic activity as these data become available.

As Tables 1 and 2 indicate, we were not successful with all subjects. This raises the question: Why does it work with some and not with others? Fortunately, in desensitization therapy, it is very easy to estimate the degree of progress in therapy. We only have to count the number of hierarchy items successfully completed. It will be recalled that all subjects received exactly eleven sessions. This meant that some people completed the hierarchy and others did not. Because each hierarchy contained twenty items (separated by subjectively equal intervals), the subject's progress was meaningfully defined by the last completed item in the eleventh session. Progress, so defined, displayed an interesting relationship to two important variables. First of all, the number of items completed was not determined by verbal or motor estimates of the subject's degree of fear of the phobic object. These people were all very much afraid, and discrimination in terms of the intensity of snake phobia was difficult.

On the other hand, there was a high correlation between the number of hierarchy items completed and positive change. Experimental subjects who passed fifteen or more items showed significant improvement on all measures of change. Subjects completing less than fifteen items could not be discriminated from control subjects. The avoidance test and "fear thermometer" results for these two groups are presented in Table 3. The findings for the snake item and total Fear Survey Schedule may be seen in Table 4.

These latter results are of particular interest. As can be seen, subjects who completed more than fifteen hierarchy items show reduced fear of snakes. However, they also report a significantly greater reduction in total Fear Survey Schedule score than subjects who fail to progress along the hierarchy. Rather than arousing new fears, as predicted by the "symptom substitution" hypotheses, successful treatment of a specific phobia appears to *reduce* other fears.

TABLE 3

Avoidance Test Behavior Change from Test 2 to Test 3 for Subjects Who Completed More than 15 Hierarchy Items, for Those Who Completed Less Than 15 Items, and Mann-Whitney Tests of Significance

Number of hierarchy items successfully completed	SNAKE AVOIDANCE SCALE			
	Test 2	Test 3	Change score	U
More than 15 (N = 7)	6.71	3.93	0.49	5.0[a]
Less than 15 (N = 6)	4.17	5.00	−0.07	
	FEAR THERMOMETER			
	Test 2	Test 3	Difference	U
More than 15 (N = 7)	7.57	4.00	3.57	8.0[b]
Less than 15 (N = 6)	7.67	6.50	1.17	

NOTE: All scores are mean values.

[a] $p < .03$
[b] $p < .08$

TABLE 4

Changes in the Fear Survey Schedule (FSS) Following Desensitization Therapy for Subjects Who Completed More than 15 Hierarchy Items, for Those Who Completed Less than 15, and Mann-Whitney Tests of Significance

Number of hierarchy items successfully completed	FEAR SURVEY SCHEDULE			
	Pre-therapy	Post-therapy	Difference	U
More than 15 (N = 7)	2.34	1.85	0.49	4.5[a]
Less than 15 (N = 6)	3.21	3.20	0.01	
	FSS-S's RATING OF SNAKE FEAR			
	Pre-therapy	Post-therapy	Difference	U
More than 15 (N = 7)	6.71	4.14	2.57	3.0[b]
Less than 15 (N = 6)	6.67	6.67	0.00	

NOTE: All scores are mean ranks or mean rank differences.

[a] $p < .02$
[b] $p < .01$

We also found a high negative correlation between success and initial score on the Fear Survey Schedule. This latter measure, in turn, correlated highly with the Taylor anxiety scale ($r = + .80$) for the experimental group. These data indicate that the more generalized a subject's anxiety, the fewer items he is able to complete, and the less positive change he shows. In other words, an important determinant of success in this time-limited therapy is the subject's over-all level of anxiety. If he was generally very anxious, the subject progressed more slowly. This is perfectly logical from the conditioning point of view. If many stimuli are capable of eliciting anxiety, more time would be necessary to counter-condition the additional connections.

It is interesting to note that anyone who completed all twenty items also touched or held the snake at the final test. Thus, there is a direct relationship between the visualization of a particular scene without anxiety and the ability actually to perform a similar behavior.

Interview data and therapist's reports suggest that further progress could have been made with many of the less successful subjects had therapy been extended beyond the eleven sessions dictated by our research design. Wolpe reported in his paper on desensitization therapy (1961) that 11.6 sessions were necessary, on the average, to treat the phobias of a patient population. Slightly over half of our experimental subjects show significant improvement in approximately the same time period. This is an encouraging similarity between clinical and laboratory findings.

As I stated previously, our experiment was repeated, using a small schizophrenic group as subjects (Cowden *et al.*, 1961). Very similar initial findings were recorded. However, the effects appeared to be more transitory. Most of the schizophrenic subjects did not maintain their gains six months after therapy. These results certainly need replication. However, Wolpe's dim predictions for the desensitization of schizophrenics may be accurate.

In addition to the FSS, the taped interviews provide further evidence against the "symptom substitution" hypothesis. None of the subjects reported symptoms in other areas of living, either immediately after therapy or at the six-month follow-up. The fact that there was little change associated with pre-therapy training, reinforces the notion that it is actual desensitization that is effecting the change, and not any simple effect of suggestion, being hypnotized, or training in muscle relaxation.

Of course, we are unable to state unequivocally that these results are attributable to "reciprocal inhibition"—the substitution of muscular relaxation for anxiety responses. We need clearer evidence on this theoretical issue. The strategy that underlies our current research involves a kind of dismantling of desensitization in order to discover the basic elements that make for success. We are, for example, eliminating hypnosis in some groups now under way. We anticipate administering the procedure without muscle relaxation training. Two subjects have recently participated in what we call "pseudo therapy." This is an atherapeutic control condition which we have invented to give us a more precise evaluation of placebo effects. It includes training in hypnosis, muscle relaxation, and hierarchy building, the same as in the experimental groups. However, in the eleven subsequent therapy sessions, these elements are employed in a way that, theoretically, should not be therapeutic. For example, deep relaxation is induced following pleasant scenes, and is not temporally related to the anxiety items. The items themselves are not presented as scenes, but are used to begin a discussion of topics remote from the phobic object. The subject, however, is given to understand that this may be effective treatment. A theory, sounding vaguely psychoanalytic, explains the procedure. Every effort is made to give the subject the same set for change that is created in desensitization therapy.

The two subjects who have already completed this experiment seemed to have been as involved in pseudo therapy, as others were in desensitization. However, neither subject showed a marked reduction in phobic behavior. More data must be collected before any conclusions are possible. Nevertheless, the procedure illustrates the special possibilities of this experimental situation. A similar method of determining base rates of change would not be possible in experiments with clinical cases.

We are also beginning to investigate the somatic changes which accompany the therapeutic process. Desensitization theory predicts that autonomic arousal and muscular tension will accompany the presentation of "anxiety hierarchy" items. The repeated presentation of a particular item should be associated with diminishing muscular and autonomic activity, and a successfully completed item should no longer elicit a tension response.

Preliminary findings support the first prediction. Increases in muscular tension and the cardiac rate, and a sharp decrease in skin resistance attend the presentation of anxiety-provoking items in the subjects we have monitored. Usually, subsequent relaxation instructions return these systems to their previous base level. However, on occasion the therapist has failed to repeat a scene which polygraph data suggested was still a stimulus for anxiety. Difficulties on the subsequent item often occurred, and it was ultimately necessary to return to the previous scene. These findings suggest that, in addition to its use in the experimental evaluation of the therapeutic process, somatic data might also be important to the therapist as a guide in actually conducting therapy. The efficiency of therapy might be considerably increased if the practitioner could refer to an oscilloscope for information about somatic indicants of arousal.

We also anticipate the utilization of polygraph recording in the evaluation of therapy outcome. Lacey (1959) has pointed out the difficulty in developing such a measure of change. Within-subject reliability sometimes seems surprisingly low. A subject's unique pattern of responses may be more important than the amplitude of any individual reaction. However, the importance of this sector of behavior warrants an effort to overcome these difficulties. Taking a lead from R. C. Davis (1957), we are studying the somatic response elicited by colored slides of the phobic object. The slides are sufficiently frightening to arouse phobic individuals, and have the advantage over the actual objects of being standard for all subjects and all presentations. Ultimately, we plan to present such materials before and after therapy.

In summary, let me say that we are very much encouraged by our results. We have some good evidence that desensitization is an effective therapy, and I think its practical application should be increased. Nevertheless, considerable work will be necessary before we have experimental support for an explanation of its effectiveness. It is this latter problem which focuses our current experiments and will determine the project's future direction.

REFERENCES

COWDEN, R. D., & FORD, L. I. Personal communication, 1961.

COWDEN, R. D., REYNOLDS, D. J., & FORD, L. I. The verbal-behavior discrepancy in schizophrenia. *J. Clin. Psychol.,* 1961, *17,* 406–408.

DAVIS, R. C., & BUCHWALD, A. M. An exploration of somatic response patterns: stimulus and sex differences. *J. comp. physiol. Psychol.,* 1957, *50,* 42–52.

JACOBSON, E. *Progressive relaxation.* Chicago: U. Chicago Press, 1938.

JONES, MARY C. A laboratory study of fear: The case of Peter. *J. gen. Psychol.,* 1924, *31,* 308–315.

KLEIN, S. Personal communication, 1961.

LACEY, J. I. Psychophysiological approaches to the evaluation of psychotherapeutic process and outcome. In E. A. Rubinstein and M. B. Parloff (Eds.), *Research in psychotherapy.* Washington, D.C.: National Pub. Co., 1959.

LANG, P. J., & LAZOVIK, A. D. The experimental desensitization of a phobia. *J. abnorm. soc. Psychol.,* 1963, *66,* 519–525.

LAZOVIK, A. D., & LANG, P. J. A laboratory demonstration of systematic desensitization psychotherapy. *J. psychol. Stud.,* 1960, *11,* 238–247.

MEYER, V. The treatment of two phobic patients on the basis of learning principles. *J. abnorm. soc. Psychol.,* 1957, *55,* 261–266.

RACHMAN, S. The treatment of anxiety and phobic reactions by systematic desensitization psychotherapy. *J. abnorm. soc. Psychol.,* 1959, *58,* 259–263.

WALK, R. D. Self ratings of fear in a fear-invoking situation. *J. abnorm. soc. Psychol.,* 1956, *52,* 171–178.

WOLPE, J. *Psychotherapy by reciprocal inhibition*. Stanford, Calif.: Stanford U. Press, 1958.

WOLPE, J. The systematic desensitization treatment of neuroses. *J. nerv. ment. Dis.,* 1961, *132,* 189–203.

DISCUSSION

Wolpe: These results, of course, are utterly fascinating to me, but before I call for discussion I would like to make two short remarks. My first thought is that the observation that the results were poor in subjects who had a lot of generalized anxiety is not surprising, because people who have generalized anxiety are very much harder to relax and you may not get such good relaxation as to bring down to zero the on-going level of anxiety. This is a matter that needs to be checked very carefully during sessions. I am not sure how carefully this was checked during these experiments, but certainly if you do not get zero anxiety, you will get very little, if any, progress in a given desensitization session.

My second remark concerns the figure of 11.6 as the mean number of sessions I have needed for desensitizing phobic hierarchies. This figure refers to the number of sessions *per* hierarchy. Very often a patient might have had two or three hierarchies, all of which would be treated during the same sessions. Suppose we had three hierarchies and used ten sessions, you would then say that for this particular patient there were 3.3 sessions per hierarchy. Actually, each hierarchy would have been treated during the ten sessions. This indicates, of course, that the total number of sessions utilized is a good deal greater than this mean figure of 11.6 reveals. In any case, only a part of a therapeutic interview is used for desensitization. To know how many scene presentations or what expenditures of time were involved in overcoming a phobia is more informative than how many sessions.

Question: How long a time interval is there between sessions, and does it make any difference?

Lang: This was allowed to vary. However, we tried to keep at least two or three days between sessions. We generally ran two a week if this was reasonably convenient for the subject and the therapist.

Question: Did it make any difference?

Lang: As far as we could see, no.

Question: Have you studied the effects of tranquilizers?

Lang: No. However, I think it is a very interesting problem. The main question is: Can the relaxation induced by a tranquilizer function as a competing response? Although I do not have any data on the issue, I suspect that relaxation must be initiated by the subject in order to be effective. When you train a person to relax, it is something he does. When you tranquilize a subject, it is something imposed on him. I think this might make a difference.

Question: What is the effect of personality features like courage or toughness?

Lang: They may contribute to differences between avoidance behavior and verbal measures of change. Some patients learn to cope more effectively with their fear. They show a clear reduction in avoidance behavior. Others seem to be more comfortable. They report less fear, but they are not any better at coping with the stimuli. The ideal patient changes in both dimensions. He becomes better able to cope, he moves closer to the animal, and he also reports that he feels less afraid. Personality factors may well determine these differences in the type and rate of change.

Question: Can you predict how different subjects will respond?

Lang: I think one of the big problems in behavior therapy is that we don't have diagnostic devices that will provide the relevant information. We need instruments, for example, that will isolate the stimuli for anxiety more rapidly than we are now able to do it. The traditional instruments don't help you much. We have had to develop our own instruments for evaluating therapeutic change.

Question: How would these techniques apply to symptoms around which there is no verbally stated anxiety—for example, character disorders?

Lang: Let me just say, generally, that if a behavior is elicited by a known stimulus, it is usually possible to train individuals to make a different response. However, desensitization is a very specific therapeutic technique, tailored to a specific behavior problem. But if your question is directed more broadly to conditioning theory, I see no reason why appropriate methods for changing the behaviors you refer to could not be worked out.

Question: What is the relation of specific phobias to generalized anxiety? Do you have any data on the desensitization of generalized anxiety?

Lang: I think, and probably Dr. Wolpe will bear me out, that the desensitization of very generalized anxiety responses is difficult, because it is hard to isolate the conditioned stimuli for anxiety. There are many things in the external surroundings that can become stimuli for anxiety, and patients may find it difficult to specify them. These may even include changes in illumination or sound level. Russian investigators have reported studies in which an externalized loop of intestine is used as the site of a conditioned stimulus. The unconditioned stimulus is electrical shock to the leg. In addition to leg withdrawal, the animal, of course, shows a generalized anxiety response, which comes to be controlled by the conditioned stimulus. This stimulus is not external, but visceral.

I see no reason why a similar mechanism might not underlie some cases of pathological anxiety in human beings. For example, the pressure exerted by partially digested food against the wall of the intestine, or a phase of peristalsis itself, could become an interoceptive conditioned stimulus for anxiety. This would result if family arguments or other emotion-arousing events consistently occurred during or following meals. Both experiments and conditioning theory suggest that such a temporal pairing, however accidental, would result in emotional distress being triggered by a phase of the digestion process. I do not believe an anxiety stimulus on the mucous wall of the small intestine is likely to be unearthed by the most thorough psychoanalysis. Frankly, this situation presents serious difficulties to any psychotherapeutic method.

Question: Since progress is more likely to occur when generalized anxiety is low, is this not another way of saying that success is more likely with normal subjects?

Lang: I would say that therapy is probably more rapid the less generalized the anxiety response. If anxiety is high, the chances are that you are not going to overcome the phobia in eleven sessions. I think Dr. Wolpe suggested the answer to this when he indicated that a single patient might have to be desensitized to many hierarchies. In the current experiment, we dealt with only one phobic response. This is, after all, a laboratory demonstration. If experimental rigor had not prevented it, we might have developed secondary hierarchies with some of our subjects. It will be useful to evaluate the effectiveness of other therapeutic methods under similar limitations of time and standardization. Dr. Arnold Lazarus of Witwatersrand University has reported some data on this issue. He found that group desensitization was much more effective in the treatment of phobias than a control therapy based on psychoanalytic principles.

Wolpe: I would like to say something more about how the problem is complicated if you have a patient with a lot of anxiety. In general, the more anxiety a person has, the more difficult the problem; but if you go into a case from a conditioning point of view, you proceed to isolate what the sources of anxiety responses are, and in a particular case, you may find yourself with three, or four, or even more specific hierarchies of stimuli that could produce anxiety. For example, you may find in one case fear in closed spaces, fear of seeing other people sick, and a fear of the trappings of death. These are three separate hierarchies. Now besides these separate hierarchies, you may also find that the person has what Dr. Lang referred to as anxiety to very pervasive stimuli, which I think is the essence of so-called free-floating anxiety. We have found that if you get a person who has anxiety just by mere virtue of exposure to such pervasive stimuli as daylight or the inside of a room, his anxiety *ipso facto* is likely to be continuous through the day. This anxiety is over and above that which can be related to specific stimuli. In a most dramatic way, in most such cases, you can dissipate this anxiety with discrete full-capacity inhalations of 70% carbon dioxide and 30% oxygen. The importance of this is that it gives you a zero starting point, in terms of anxiety, for your desensitization session during which you will introduce the stimuli specific to your hierarchy. I have treated many cases of very extensive and very severe neuroses, which, by this systematic approach, have been overcome, as far as I can tell, in every respect.

BEHAVIOR THERAPY USING HYPNOSIS

A. Hussain, M.D.

In the past few years a new form of therapy called "behavior therapy" has emerged in the field of psychotherapy. Based on modern learning theory, its clinical application has given better results than other forms of psychotherapy. In psychoneurotic and related behavior disorders it gives favorable results in 90 percent of cases, compared with 50 percent for traditional methods of psychotherapy (Wolpe, 1958).

The writer has treated 105 patients, mostly as out-patients, with techniques classifiable with those of Wolpe under the general heading "psychotherapy by reciprocal inhibition." Reconditioning, in cases of deficit autonomic responses, and deconditioning, in cases of surplus autonomic and motor responses, were both achieved with the help of hypnosis. New conditioned responses were built up during the trance state to verbal cues, based on experimental evidence that conditioning is facilitated under hypnosis (Das, 1961; Kaufman, 1961). The writer has also observed that *inhibition* of various responses can be easily achieved during the trance state.

GENERAL APPROACH

The patients were not specially selected for this form of psychotherapy. They were referred mostly by family physicians for outpatient psychiatric consultation. A full history of the patients was taken, and a complete physical examination was done to rule out the possibility of any organic illness. No facilities were available for psychometric tests. Various environmental factors that might have contributed to the formation of the symptom complex were also noted. Patients were classified according to the "dimensions of personality" suggested by Eysenck (1957). It was hypothesized, in line with this classification, that extroverts would be difficult to condition as compared with introverts.

All psychotics were excluded from this therapy. The range of cases treated is shown in Table 1.

TABLE 1

Clinical diagnosis	No. of patients
1. Anxiety reactions:	
a. Chronic with somatic complaints	50
b. With phobic and panic attacks	
2. Obsessive-compulsive neuroses	2
3. Hysterical reaction:	
a. Dissociative	
b. With somatic manifestations— paralysis, aphonia, etc.	15
4. Sociopathic personality disturbance	3
5. Behavior disorders of children, age 6–14 years, including school phobia	10
6. Psychosomatic disorders:	
a. Chronic eczema	3
b. Speech disorders	3
c. Asthma	3
d. Eczema-asthma syndrome	1
e. Incontinence of urine or feces	5
f. Diarrhea	3
g. Sexual disorders:	
a. Frigidity	
b. Dyspareunia	7
c. Psychic impotence	
TOTAL	105

METHOD OF TREATMENT

During the first interview a list was made of various neurotic reactions, which were ranked in order of severity. The patient's response to hypnosis was also tested. Therapeutic sessions that lasted from thirty minutes to one hour were held once weekly. The length of time taken for the therapy varied from four to sixteen weeks.

The main therapeutic procedure employed was a derivative[1] of the desensitization based on relaxation described by Wolpe (1958). The case histories that follow, and especially Case 1, illustrate some of the details of the method, as well as the variety of syndromes.

CASE HISTORIES

Case 1

A thirty-five-year-old white divorced woman, having one child, a girl aged five, was admitted to the hospital as a voluntary patient. The social history disclosed that the patient had been drinking excessively for the past eight years, and had been feeling depressed and suicidal. She was also sexually promiscuous while under the effects of alcohol. The patient had a master's degree. She came from a middle-class family. Her mother was considered to be an anxiety-prone individual, and had needed psychiatric treatment. The patient was the youngest child and had been thoroughly spoiled when young. The mother was demanding and overprotective.

The patient had married a well-known scientist when she was twenty-seven. Her husband's excessive preoccupation with his work, and the fame and honor he received, caused her to feel unloved and neglected. Also, she was a poor housekeeper, and the strain of being a housewife started her drinking, first socially, then regularly. She had frequent quarrels with her husband, and attempted suicide twice. The birth of the child worsened the situation, and ultimately she was divorced. Following this, she drank continually and was fired from her job. She was hospitalized on many occasions without showing any improvement.

When referred for individual psychotherapy, she had already been in the hospital for a few weeks. She had no ambition and was feeling depressed and suicidal. She did not want to leave the hospital.

Her list of symptoms was as follows:

a. Feeling of panic when thinking of her marriage
b. Anxiety when meeting with her mother
c. Feelings of inadequacy and anxiety at thought of looking after her daughter
d. Anxiety at having to accept authority

---

[1] The reader will observe that Dr. Hussain's method is distinctly different from the desensitization technique. In the latter, the patient is given preliminary training in relaxation, the fear-evoking stimuli are placed in hierarchical order after being thematically grouped, and treatment involves exposure to *gradually* stronger stimuli. See Wolpe (pp. 11–12) and Lang (pp. 39–41). [Editor's note.]

    e. Worry over her sexual promiscuity (producing insomnia)

    f. Inability to make decisions or future plans

Therapy Sessions:

First Session:

    Hypnotic trance was induced by the eye-fixation technique. The patient's suggestibility was tested by hand levitation, and also later on by posthypnotic suggestion. As the patient proved to be quite suggestible, general suggestions of deep relaxation were given. She was allowed to express her feelings, whether she felt relaxed or not. When she felt relaxed, she was given posthypnotic suggestions of deep relaxation during the waking state. Though no direct deconditioning was initiated, still the relaxation responses inhibited the anxiety responses reciprocally. Afterwards she felt relaxed and happy for the first time during this week.

Second Session:

    The patient stated that she had felt relaxed most of the time during the past week. However, she still felt upset by the thought of married life, her mother, and so on. Now she was again placed in the trance state, and given suggestions to think without anxiety of incidents during her marriage. Finally she was given posthypnotic suggestions that she would henceforth be relaxed on thinking of her marriage.

Third Session:

    Patient stated that she had been feeling quite relaxed and cheerful. She had been discussing her married life with other female patients for the first time. She felt relaxed and had no feelings of anxiety. She was again placed in a trance and previous suggestions were reinforced. Then she was asked to think about her mother without becoming upset, and was able to do so.

    Between the fourth and twelfth sessions her anxieties were similarly overcome in relation to her daughter, people in authority, her sexual promiscuity, and situations requiring decisions. Aversion to the thought and sight of alcohol was also built up by direct suggestion. After the twelfth session she was discharged from the hospital. She had obtained a job and was looking forward to it.

    The patient came three times in the next three months. She stated that she had accidentally discovered that her employer was a chronic alcoholic and was in the habit of drinking secretly. Though he had coerced her to drink a little with him, she had refused. She felt disgusted with alcohol and did not want to touch even a drop of it. About her home life, she informed me that two persons had been trying to date her, but she had been hesitant as she wanted a husband and not a lover. When later she found a person who had honorable intentions of marriage, she allowed a sexual relationship to develop.

    In the next three months she phoned to inform me that she was doing well, and had established a firm relationship with her "boy friend." Her general efficiency was good. She had no difficulty in refusing drinks from her friends. She was now seeing more of her daughter and mother without getting upset and nervous. She was sleeping well without the help of sleeping pills.

Once the patient was successfully deconditioned to the previous anxiety-provoking stimuli, her increased productivity and efficiency at her work and better interpersonal relationships were noticed by her parents and friends.

One would be justified in considering this case as one of radical cure, as no relevant symptoms were left behind and there was no relapse during the six-month follow-up period.

Case 2

An eighteen-year-old single girl was admitted to the hospital for anti-social behavior. The parents reported that she had been drinking heavily for the last three years and associating with criminals and ex-convicts. She was known for her violent temper, and had often threatened to kill her parents. She had a complete disregard for law and was involved in a number of antisocial incidents with some shady friends.

She was the eldest child and had shown a stubborn streak since an early age. Subsequently she began running away from school and staying out late. Her parents were quite unable to control her.

She responded well to hypnosis. Her responses of rebelliousness and anger were reciprocally inhibited by relaxation responses. During the trance state, verbal cues and posthypnotic suggestions, responses of relaxation and obedience to law and authority were built up. In six weeks she was a changed girl, who for the first time started reacting to environmental situations in a mature way. She got a job as a secretary. She was also soon after able to live with her parents without aggressive behavior. She was discharged from treatment after twelve weeks. She was followed up for nine months, during which she was doing well and had no problems.

Case 3

A forty-five-year-old white married male was referred for my opinion. He complained of inability to relax or sleep, as he would get sudden attacks of panic. He had been unable to work for the past five years. His history disclosed that his symptoms had started when he was injured on the left hand during World War II, when a booby trap he was setting accidentally exploded.

He responded well to hypnosis, and when relaxed was made to relive this situation. When he started crying, deep relaxation responses were suggested. He showed progressive improvement and was discharged after eight weeks. As there was no recurrence of symptoms of panic and anxiety he went into employment. He has had no relapse during one and a half years.

Case 4

A thirty-five-year-old white male and his thirty-four-year-old wife were both referred for psychiatric opinion, since they had been married for ten years and no sexual intercourse had taken place. The wife suffered from dyspareunia, anxiety, and various somatic complaints. The husband was alleged by the wife to be impotent.

Both were treated by hypnosis. During the trance, the wife's anxiety was inhibited by relaxation responses. Later on she was advised to try vaginal dilators for building up confidence. The husband was also treated with relaxation responses. The anxiety responses in both were inhibited, and for the first time in ten years, sexual union resulted. Both were overjoyed with the effects of the treatment, which took eight weeks altogether. No symptom substitution took place, and they have continued to enjoy married life as never before.

RESULTS

Recovery was assessed objectively on the basis of the direct observations of the writer and the comments of relatives, as well as subjectively on the patients' increased feelings of well-being and reports of increased productiveness, ability to handle difficult situations, and improvement in interpersonal relationships. The patients were regarded as their own controls, in view of the brevity of the treatment.

The over-all recovery rate (in terms of complete or almost complete removal of symptoms) was 95.2 percent. Of the five patients who failed to respond, two prematurely terminated therapy; two did not show any response, and had not shown response to other forms of therapy; and one was prepsychotic and was later admitted to the hospital for psychotic depression.

In follow-ups ranging from six months to two years no instance of relapse or symptom-substitution was noted.

These results are obviously superior to those that have been reported for other forms of therapy (Eysenck, 1952), though the latter are often much more time-consuming and expensive.

DISCUSSION

This study presents evidence that confirms the effectiveness of conditioning therapy in the treatment of neurotic patients and the durability of the results obtained, in line with earlier studies (Salter, 1949; Raymond,

1956; Lazarus & Rachman, 1957; Jones, 1958; Wolpe, 1958; Bond & Hutchison, 1960; Eysenck, 1960; Moss, 1960; Rachman, 1961).

In the course of this therapy it was noted by the writer that the deconditioning techniques were made more effective by the help of hypnosis. It was observed that deep relaxation responses reciprocally inhibited the anxiety responses. Not only was conditioning facilitated during the trance state, but deficit responses were also built up more easily.

Eysenck (1957) has pointed out that sociopaths and hysterics have deficits of conditioned responses. The writer was successful in reconditioning some of them to a socially acceptable standard of behavior, but, as Eysenck predicted, they were more difficult to condition than dysthymic subjects.

Eysenck's statement (1960) that getting rid of the symptom cures the neurosis has also been verified by this study. After the removal of symptoms, no evidence was found of deep conflicts left behind. If neurotic behavior were an outcome of strong repression over the id impulses, then, after symptom removal, the basic conflicts should have remained. Since evidence of such conflicts was not encountered even in a single case, it is difficult to believe that the psychoanalytic theories of psychoneurosis are valid.

Behavior therapy has been criticized on the *a priori* ground that symptom removal must be followed by symptom substitution, and that therefore it is a superficial form of therapy. The writer has not encountered a single case of symptom substitution.

It has also been said that behavior therapy will precipitate psychoses. This theory has not been borne out clinically. One can only say that those occasional patients who develop acute psychosis have probably not been screened properly and have been misdiagnosed. On a number of occasions I have seen cases of early schizophrenia presenting as acute anxiety reactions and being treated as neurotic. Such patients are liable to develop florid psychoses during any form of psychotherapy, and are probably equally liable to do so without therapy.

Wolpe's principle of psychotherapy by reciprocal inhibition was confirmed clinically by the results achieved. However, in cases with deficit conditioned responses one had to introduce another form of therapy, and build up new responses by positive conditioning, as Rachman (1961) has suggested might be necessary.

It is important to point out that with this treatment all of a person's neurotic responses are eliminated. In some patients with more than one symptom, elimination of one may increase the prominence of others until they also are removed. This is clearly not to be regarded as symptom substitution.

SUMMARY

In this paper the writer has described how he has found confirmation of the theories of Eysenck and Wolpe in a different clinical usage. The vast variety of conditions successfully treated (95.2 percent recovery rate) supports the idea that their view of therapy is the correct one for neuroses. As the results were apparently lasting, one is reinforced in the belief that the basis of neurotic behavior is not repression and various complexes, but rather simple lack of conditioning or overconditioning by environmental situations, both being learned unadaptive patterns of behavior. The proposition, "anything that can be learned can be unlearned," has been borne out by this study.

REFERENCES

BOND, I. K., & HUTCHISON, H. C. The application of reciprocal inhibition therapy to exhibitionism. *Canad. M.A.J.,* 1960, *83,* 23–25.

DAS, J. P. Learning and recall under hypnosis and in the waking state. *Arch. gen. Psychiat.,* 1961, *4,* 517–521.

EYSENCK, H. J. The effects of psychotherapy: An evaluation. *J. consult. Psychol.,* 1952, *16,* 319–324.

EYSENCK, H. J. *The dynamics of anxiety and hysteria.* London: Routledge, 1957.

EYSENCK, H. J. *Behaviour therapy and the neuroses.* New York: Pergamon, 1960.

JONES, H. G. Neurosis and experimental psychology. *J. ment. Sci.,* 1958, *104,* 55–62.

KAUFMAN, M. Hypnosis in psychotherapy today. *Arch. gen. Psychiat.,* 1961, *4,* 30–56.

LAZARUS, A., & RACHMAN, S. The use of systematic desensitization in psychotherapy. *S. African Med. J.,* 1957, *31,* 934–937.

MOSS, C. S. Brief successful psychotherapy of a chronic phobic reaction. *J. abnorm. soc. Psychol.,* 1960, *60,* 266–270.

RAYMOND, M. J. Case of fetishism treated by aversion therapy. *Brit. Med. J.,* 1956, *2,* 854–857.

RACHMAN, S. Sexual disorders and behaviour therapy. *Amer. J. Psychiat.,* 1961, *118,* 235–240.

SALTER, A. *Conditioned reflex therapy.* New York: Farrar, Straus, 1949; Capricorn Books—Putnam's Sons, 1961.

WOLPE, J. *Psychotherapy by reciprocal inhibition.* Stanford: Stanford U. Press, 1948.

SOME APPLICATIONS OF OPERANT CONDITIONING TO BEHAVIOR THERAPY

Arthur J. Bachrach, Ph.D

INTRODUCTION

Before I get into the consideration of some of the applications of operant conditioning to behavior therapy I would like to make a few general comments about behaviorism and psychoanalysis, in particular, the areas of agreement and disagreement, as I view them. I do not intend to dwell on the scientific and metaphysical aspects of the difference between these two systems, but will content myself with presenting a brief comparison and comments. I think the major differences are in *methodology*. Among these are the following: Psychoanalysis deals with inferences about "inner" behavior, interprets, and symbolizes. Behaviorism deals with observable motor activity, minimizes interpretation, and demands specification of operations. To place these in a tabular form, let me first present the points of departure between psychoanalysis and behaviorism and then the points of agreement.

POINTS OF DEPARTURE

PSYCHOANALYSIS	BEHAVIORISM
Philosophical heritage: ideas, will, personality; dualistic (mind as distinct from body), mental apparatus	Biological heritage: muscles, glands, effectors; monistic (mind as physiological response), observable action
Emphasis on inner causes of behavior	Emphasis on environmental events controlling behavior
Inferential and interpretative symbols	Operational response
Emphasis on individual	Study of individual but emphasis on general laws of behavior

POINTS OF AGREEMENT:

Importance of observing behavior
Acceptance of cause-effect relationship (behavior not whimsical)
Lawful determinism of behavior
Importance of understanding history of individual and his learning experiences
From this, relation of past events to current behavior
Acceptance of genetic, constitutional factors as relevant

Some characteristics of operant conditioning as a behavioral system

Behavioristic systems, in general, rely on an emphasis on the accurate description of behavior and of the methodologies involved in the manipulation of behavior. Of the characteristics fairly specific to operant conditioning, there are two which I believe are of major importance; these are, first, the *emphasis on the individual* and, second, the *free operant.* The emphasis on the individual is in contrast with the most frequently used approach in psychological research—the use of group data. In the experimental analysis of behavior, as represented by operant conditioning, the individual is the subject of systematic research. Operant conditioning, originally propounded by Skinner (1938), has developed along these lines. Sidman (1956), in a discussion of Skinner's work, offers the following comment:

> Skinner's rejection of "confidence level statistics" derives from his clearly stated interest in the behavior of the individual. This interest dictates an experimental design different from that generally used in psychology. Instead of running groups of animals and averaging their data, it becomes necessary to run individual animals through all of the experimental manipulations. Each animal thus constitutes a replication of the experiment, which not only affords an opportunity for detecting differences among animals, but also actually imposes the obligation to report them and, where possible, to *explain* them. The procedure of treating differences among animals as lawful, rather than as examples of the capriciousness of nature or of the experimental techniques, provides Skinner with one of his substitutes for statistical treatment. Experimentation is continued until the variables responsible for "deviant" behavior are identified. A corollary of this point of view is that any behavioral effect repeatedly demonstrated in the same animal is a lawful phenomenon.

Inasmuch as the central focus of behavior therapy is with the individual, the systematic replication with the single individual provides more information and more control than grouping data can possibly do. This is not an argument against group data, but merely a suggestion that behavioral manipulation occurs most reliably and most systematically with individuals. It also does away with a mythical average, a concept which is not entirely useful in clinical behavioral manipulation.

The concept of the *free operant* tends to differentiate operant conditioning from classical, or respondent, conditioning in that it works with an organism theoretically free to respond or not to respond under certain environmental conditions. As Ferster (1953) observes, "the use of the free operant is a method of wide generality; it refers to any apparatus that generates a response which takes a short time to occur and leaves the animal in the same place ready to respond again. The free operant is used in experiments when the main dependent variable is the frequency of occurrence of behavior." He further observes that almost all the problems encountered in a science of behavior fit this paradigm when one asks the questions, What is the likelihood of a piece of behavior occurring on this particular occasion? How strong is the tendency to behave on this occasion relative to another occasion? The concept of response frequency will be considered in more detail below. At the moment, I would like only to observe that when an animal is free to respond it allows for a *shaping* of behavior, beginning with perhaps diffuse and exploratory responding. We might also suggest that it helps eliminate some of the artifacts engendered by apparatus in a classical conditioning experiment. Liddell and Gantt have pointed out in their writings that one of the crucial factors in the development of experimental neuroses in the Pavlovian conditioning techniques was the harness in which the animal was strapped. By keeping the organism free-moving the problems engendered by immobilization and restriction of activity are minimized or eliminated.

The specification of response and stimulus

Fundamental to any behavioristic system is the recognition of the necessity for the clear specification of the behavior to be studied and controlled. As I have suggested earlier, one of the difficulties with a "psychodynamic" approach to behavior is that it does not clearly specify the responses demanded of the individual, because its terminology is couched in the abstract and uses indirect behavioral descriptions or inferences such as "ego-strength" or "depression." Whereas the psychoanalytic therapist may attempt to "build up the ego-strength of his patient," the conditioner, in his experimental manipulations, must be more specific about the responses with which he is working. So we begin with the specification of the response. The experimenter must indicate what he wishes the individual, whose behavior he is manipulating, to do. In animal experimentation, for example, this may be simply set in terms such as the requirement that a pigeon peck at a translucent plastic key a total of 50 times before he is rewarded by the presentation of food. On a more complex human level the demands for specification are no less real and no less important.

An example of this may be drawn from a recent case of *anorexia nervosa* treated by operant conditioning techniques by W. J. Erwin, Jay Mohr, and myself. A complete report of the medical and experimental psychological aspects of this case is in press (1964). For the moment, let me draw upon one illustration from this individual's situation. By definition, this patient was a person who ate with a frequency significantly below her usual frequency, and certainly, in group terms, critically below normal frequency. Without resorting to such unproved explanatory concepts as the "fear of oral impregnation" or, indeed, without any primary consideration of factors which had been involved in her initial cessation of eating, we specified the response we desired simply as an increase in the frequency of food intake, with its concomitant increase in the amount of ingested food. Inasmuch as it was obvious that the eating response and food did not have their expected reinforcing characteristics for this individual, the case was studied to learn what reinforcement *would* be significant to her. We found that she enjoyed visits from people, music, reading, and television, and was accordingly placed on deprivation for all of these. She was put in a barren room and the presentation of visitors, records, television, or books was made contingent upon eating and weight gain. Time does not permit a full account of this case but, as I have noted, such an account is in preparation. The main point to be drawn from this illustration is that there was no need to resort to inferential explanations of her behavior, but there *was* a clear need to specify what it was we demanded of her, as well as the conditions under which the eating response could be manipulated and increased in frequency. I might add that after a little over a year of such operant conditioning control of her behavior both in and out of the hospital situation, she has more than doubled her initial experimental weight of 47 pounds and is continuing to add weight. I think this emphasis on the specification of behavior is central to the system of psychotherapy based on the principle of reciprocal inhibition expounded by Wolpe (1958).

Although the specification of the response may be a relatively simple matter in the experimental control of behavior, the specification of the *stimulus* is not so simple. Indeed, it may become inferential. We can usually only guess as to the stimuli which evoke or set the occasion for behavior, and so one of the tenets of operant conditioning is that it is more effective to start with a response which is observable, measurable, and manipulable and to consider that the relationship of

$$\text{Response} \longrightarrow \text{Reinforcement}$$

is the critical one.

We may begin with the assumption that stimulating conditions are always involved in an organism's response, but by far the clearer datum with which we can work is the response itself, and those consequences upon the response which alter the future likelihood of that response's recurrence. "Reinforcement" is the term generally applied to the consequences of a response; one of the best definitions of reinforcement is that offered by Sidman (1960): "Any event, contingent upon the response of the organism that alters the future likelihood of that response." By definition, positive reinforcement (usually termed loosely a "reward") is any event likely to increase the probability of the response's recurring, whereas a negative reinforcement (loosely a "punishment") is any event that tends to decrease the probability of that response's recurrence, although some procedural differentiation must be made.

Beginning with a suggestion of Goldiamond's, Thompson (1962) has developed a model to differentiate types of reinforcement and their relationship to response probability (or its empirical counterpart, response frequency).

Stimulus event / *Response probability*	*Presentation*		A) *Termination* B) *Postponement*
	Contingent upon response	Noncontingent upon response	Contingent upon response
Increase	Positive reinforcement Fixed interval Fixed ratio Variable interval Variable ratio	Superstitious behavior	Negative reinforcement A) Escape B) Avoidance
Decrease	Punishment	Conditioned suppression	A) Extinction B) Differentiated reinforcement of low rates (DRL)

The reinforcement contingencies in a free-operant situation are those conditions (temporal, intensive, and topographical) under which a response is closely followed by an environmental consequence. Schedules of reinforcement, or programmed contingencies, may be *procedurally* delineated into six classes on the basis of response probability as a function of stimulus events.

To illustrate, using the above schema, "punishment" is defined as the *presentation* of a *stimulus event, contingent upon the response,* which produces a *decrease* in *response probability.* Conversely, "negative reinforcement" (escape) is defined as the termination of a stimulus event, contingent upon the response, which produces an increase in response probability. Thus, punishment might be a shock that is delivered to a rat only when he presses a bar. Similarly, if the shock is on all the time, except when a bar press terminates it for a specific duration, an escape contingency is in effect. The remaining schedules may be differentiated in a similar fashion.

Using the concept of response frequency allows us to approach our data with greater clarity. An example of this is found in the work on brain stimulation reported by Olds and Milner (1954). They discovered that electrical stimulation of the septal area of the brain was reinforcing to a rat. The original and quite logical hypothesis was that if electric shock delivered to a rat's feet through a grid on the floor of the cage was "punishing," then electric shock delivered directly to the rat's brain would, perhaps, be more punishing. This did not prove to be the case. A rat punished for entering a certain corner of a box, by the delivery of a shock to his septal area, increased his movement toward that corner. Using our definition of positive reinforcement as any event that increases the probability of a response's recurring, then we must say that electrical stimulation of the brain was positively reinforcing; hence it was not at all punishing, but, on the contrary, rewarding. The excellent work of the last few years reported by other investigators, such as Brady (1962), supports the evidence that electrical stimulation of the brain under certain conditions is positively reinforcing. Although it is certainly possible to use an explanatory fiction such as "masochism" to explain why a rat or other animal (cats, dogs, monkeys, and other organisms have been used in these experiments) will deliver electrical stimulation to his own brain when given an opportunity to operate a manipulandum to do this, it is simpler and much more effective to note the relationship of electrical stimulation and increased responding, and to work from there.

Response frequency

Throughout this paper I have been referring to the concept of response frequency, which is basic to operant conditioning. The frequency with which a response is emitted is the clearest datum with which a psychologist can work, and, as noted above in the use of the free operant, experiments are designed to allow the animal to make a response and be ready to respond again. Elsewhere (1962a) I have referred to the fact that descriptions of behavior are very often expressed in terms which have an underlying response frequency, referring to the observations of Skinner (1953) that to describe a person as "hostile" or as "an enthusiastic skier" or as "an inveterate gambler" is clearly to denote the frequency of a particular response class. The "enthusiastic skier" skis a lot. The "inveterate gambler" gambles with frequency. In short, what is often used as a "personality" description is simply a reference to a particular frequent response class as observed by others.

Shaping

If the operant conditioner, approaching an organism in an experimental space, specifies the response he desires from the organism and the frequency with which he wishes this response emitted, he is in a position to shape the organism's behavior. In the establishment of behavior the experimenter begins with the mass of responses available to the organism he is manipulating. Sidman (1960) offers an example of shaping behavior:

> Shaping is accomplished by reinforcing successively closer approximations to the behavior with which the experimenter ultimately wants to work. The experimental situation, for example, may be one in which a monkey is to be reinforced with food for pressing a lever. If the monkey just sits quietly at first, the experimenter will wait until the animal moves and will then immediately deliver the food. By continuing to reinforce all movements, the experimenter will soon have an active animal with which to work. He then reinforces only those responses which bring the animal closer to the lever, as if drawn by an invisible string. The experimenter now directs his attention to the animal's hand. He delivers the food whenever the hand moves closer to the lever, and it is not long before the animal places its hand on the lever and depresses it. The experimenter can then turn the rest of the job over to his automatic apparatus, which will deliver the food only when the animal actually depresses the lever.

We may modify some of the rules suggested by Sidman in the establishment of behavior through shaping. A basic rule is to reinforce the behavior immediately. "If the reinforcement is delayed even by a fraction of a second, it is likely to be preceded by some behavior other than that which the experimenter intended to reinforce." It is also critical that the experimenter not give too many or too few reinforcements for an approximation of the desired final response. As Sidman observes, "Behavior that is initially reinforced must ultimately be extinguished as we move closer to the end point. If we reinforce intermediate forms of behavior too much, these once-reinforced but now-to-be-discarded responses will continue to intrude and will unduly prolong the shaping process." And, from the other standpoint, there is the risk that an experimenter may abandon a response "before he has reinforced it enough and, as a consequence, both the response and the variations which stem from it extinguish before he can mold the next closer approximation to the final behavior. The subject may then return to his original behavior, as if he had never gone through a shaping process at all." Sidman notes, at this point, that it is often tempting to refer to an animal who does not respond "correctly" as being "stupid." It is tempting also for us to consider that the therapist may refer to a patient as being "resistant" if his therapeutic manipulations prove unsuccessful. Many proponents of the experimental analysis of behavior feel that "the organism is always right," and that if we were able to know the reinforcement history of the subject, his physiological condition, and the environmental stimulus conditions under which he is performing we could probably assume that his behavior (while perhaps maladjusted in the eyes of others) is appropriate to his own situation.

A final rule which Sidman suggests is one basic to the present discussion:

> *Carefully specify the response to be reinforced in each successive step.* Before abandoning one response and reinforcing the next approximation to the final behavior, the experimenter must watch the subject closely to determine what behavior is available for reinforcement. He should then specify that behavior as quantitatively as possible and adhere rigorously to the specification he has established. Otherwise he may inadvertently reinforce a slightly different but highly undesirable form of response and unnecessarily prolong the shaping process.

Let me turn now to an example of the shaping of complex behavior, with an illustration drawn from laboratory work.

COMPLEX BEHAVIOR

Several years ago a team of psychologists at Barnard College, under the direction of Drs. Rosemary Pierrel and J. Gilmour Sherman, set up a demonstration of complex behavioral chaining in a white rat. We have modified this demonstration for the same purpose, to demonstrate that complex behavior may be conditioned, response by response, to form a final "fluid" response chain. Our rat, S. R. Rodent, is reinforced by the presentation of food in a tray following bar pressing. But before he can get to press the bar to receive his pellets, Rodent has to climb a spiral staircase, run across a drawbridge, climb a ladder, get into a cable car and pull himself across a gap a couple of feet above the floor of his box, climb another stairway, play a toy piano (hitting two keys of eight which activate a switch, the switch opening a crossing gate from a model railroad), run through the tunnel when the crossing gate is open, climb into an elevator, pull a chain to release the elevator, ride down to the bottom floor and then press his bar to receive his pellets. This chain of responses is demonstrated in Figures 1 through 10. I might add, parenthetically, that this behavior is extremely reinforcing to the experimenter.

But we did not set up this demonstration purely for our own amusement. We did it because we wished to show that at each particular stage the behavior of the organism is specifically conditioned. The impression while watching S. R. Rodent run through all these paces (which he does in approximately 15 seconds) is that his is a fluid single motion, but he wasn't trained that way. For one thing he was trained "backward." First, he was trained to the tray approach, i.e., to become accustomed to eating his pellets in the tray of the food magazine. Then he was trained to press the bar to deliver the pellet. Next he was shaped to elevator riding to get down to the bar to press it for the pellet. Next, to pull the chain to release the elevator so that he could ride down, and so on. At each individual stage of the shaping, the desired response was achieved by approximation techniques. For example, to oversimplify one illustration, the most difficult response of getting him to pull the chain to release the elevator was accomplished by getting him to make movements toward the chain—to sniff it, to touch it with his nose, then his paws, and finally to pull it. Each one of these was an approximation toward the final desired response of chain pulling. The obvious advantage of training "backward" is that each response becomes not only a cue (or discriminative stimulus) for the immediate and succeeding response, but also a secondary reinforcement for the preceding one. Pressing the piano key, for example, sets the occasion for a click associated with the opening of the crossing gate, making the tunnel accessible to his running.

There are, of course, implications for human learning in S. R. Rodent's behavior. In the shaping of skills, for example, such as tennis strokes or the operation of a motor vehicle, the final fluidity of the action is not like the original training in which a chain of separate responses was individually shaped. Admittedly leaping generalizations, I think that there are implications also for psychotherapy. I don't believe that the abstract conceptual approach to psychotherapy is as effective as the clear delineation of therapist and patient behavior, involving the responses of both persons in the interaction, and the cue or discriminative stimuli occasioning these responses. It is for this reason, I think, that Hans Strupp (1962), who is certainly a good psychodynamic therapist, has said that he feels that the outcome studies are probably not as useful in psychotherapy as process studies which help focus on what is actually occurring in the immediate therapeutic situation. Learning the significant discriminative stimuli and the differentiated responses clearly specified at each appropriate step should provide a great deal more information about psychotherapy than will abstract theoretical formulations of psychodynamics.

I would like now to report two experiments that have been accomplished using operant conditioning techniques on psychiatric patients. What happens, obviously, is that we no longer have complete control of the experimental subjects as we do with S. R. Rodent, or as we have with pigeons or monkeys in an experimental situation. With our animals we can control deprivation and reinforcement, we can control the actual manipulation of the organism in the experimental space, but in the "real life" situation on a psychiatric ward such control is necessarily limited. I've always liked a term proposed by Egon Brunswik—"representative design"—which suggests that the ideal experiment is one that has a minimum of artificiality and a maximum of control. Ideally, if we can get a cross-over point where experimental controls are still rigorous, and yet the problem with which we are working is close to the real-life situation, we would have representative design. This problem has been attacked in some detail in recent volumes (Bachrach, 1962b, 1962c).

I would like to report first an experiment accomplished by Ayllon and Michael (1959), who analyzed the ward behavior of psychiatric patients and concluded that many of the ward problems presented by these patients resulted directly from the reinforcement setting in the hospital. They concerned themselves primarily with the behavior of the patients on the ward that might become "so persistent that it engages the full energies of the nurses, and postpones, sometimes permanently, any effort on their part to deal with the so-called basic problem." They were referring to such behaviors as "failures to eat, dress, bathe, interact socially with other patients and walk without being led, hoarding various objects, hitting, pinching, spitting on other patients, constant attention-seeking actions with respect to the nurses, upsetting chairs in the dayroom, scraping paint from the walls, breaking windows, stuffing paper in the mouth and ears. . . ."

As an example of the extinction of such undesirable behavior, the nurses were able to withhold reinforcement of patients' responses of habitually entering the nurse's office. Such behavior had obviously been

Figure 1

Figure 2

Figure 3

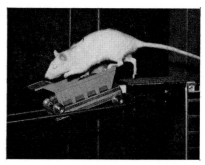

Figure 4

Figure 5

Figure 6

Figure 7

Figure 8

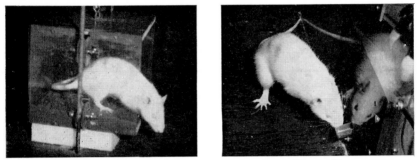

Figure 9   Figure 10

reinforced by the nurse's responding (even though it might have been with annoyance) to patients entering the nurse's office. By ignoring this behavior the nurses were able to reduce the incidence to a point where it was no longer disturbing their routine duties.

Another technique used in the study is reminiscent of Wolpe's reciprocal inhibition. They reinforced incompatible behavior in a patient who was violent. In two patients, who consistently refused to eat unless they were aided by the ward nurses, escape and avoidance conditioning techniques were used. Both patients were also extremely concerned with neatness and with keeping their clothes clean, and the nurse began the practice of spilling food on the patients' clothing whenever they insisted on being spoon-fed. This negatively reinforcing spilling could be avoided if the patients fed themselves. In both cases the result was the desired response of self-feeding.

In a similar series of experiments, conducted by Ayllon and Haughton (1962), the experimenters found that approximately 50 percent of the schizophrenic patients on a ward presented food problems. The subject population consisted of 45 psychiatric patients, 91 per cent of whom were long-term schizophrenics. The eating behavior of the approximately 50 percent of this population that had a history of refusal to eat had remained relatively unaffected by one or more of these techniques: spoon-feeding, tube-feeding, intravenous feeding, and electroshock. All aids to feeding the patients were discontinued. The patients in one experiment were left alone at mealtimes, and had to go into the dining room to eat. Next the level of complexity was raised so that the patient could not eat unless she appeared in the dining room within thirty minutes after a nurse called dinner (a discriminative stimulus). The doors would then be locked and the patient would miss that particular meal. Successful establishment of self-feeding in the social dining room situation was achieved.

In another related experiment the investigators set up a chain of responses after the eating was under control. "The patients were required to drop a penny into the slot of a collection can to gain entrance to the dining room. In addition, access to the dining room was limited to 5 minutes from the time of meal call. The development of the coin as S^D [discriminative stimulus] for entering the dining room was begun by having a nurse distribute a penny to each of the patients congregated outside the dining room at meal time." By other shaping techniques the motor response required to obtain food reinforcement was learned by all the schizophrenic patients. Other experimental controls were used and the authors conclude that "studies using schizophrenics attribute their frequently impaired performance to underlying intellectual, perceptual or sensory deficits. The data reported in this paper demonstrate that the control of psychotic behavior depends largely on the use of strong reinforcers." Evidence is clearly presented in these experiments that the schizophrenic "out of touch with reality" can be controlled behaviorally if the environmental conditions and manipulations are properly established.

There have been other experimental programs, such as Lindsley's (1960), in which more experimentally controlled techniques were used with psychotic patients, and Ellis, Barnett, and Pryer's (1960) work on mental defectives. All the experiments with the patients have followed the general principles of operant conditioning, with necessary modifications. Accepting the principle of the lawfulness of behavior, we can be confident and hopeful that the techniques of operant conditioning developed in the laboratory can ultimately be applied to behavior therapy with as much success as is demonstrated in experimental animals.

REFERENCES

AYLLON, T., & MICHAEL, J. The psychiatric nurse as a behavioral engineer. *J. exp. Anal. Behav.*, 1959, *2*, 323–334.

AYLLON, T., & HAUGHTON, E. Control of the behavior of schizophrenic patients by food. *J. exp. Anal. Behav.*, 1962, *5*, 343–352.

BACHRACH, A. J. An experimental approach to superstitious behavior. *J. Am. Folklore*, 1962, *75*, 1–9(a).

BACHRACH, A. J. (Ed.) *Experimental foundations of clinical psychology.* New York: Basic, 1962(b).

BACHRACH, A. J. *Psychological research.* New York: Random House, 1962(c).

BACHRACH, A. J. Operant conditioning and behavior: Some clinical aplications. In H. Lief, N. Lief, & V. Lief (Eds.) *The psychological basis of medical practice.* New York: Harper, 1963.

BACHRACH, A. J., ERWIN, W. J., and MOHR, J. P. The control of eating behavior in an anorexic by operant conditioning techniques. In L. Ullman and L. Krasner (Eds.) *Case studies in behavior modification,* New York: Holt, Rinehart and Winston, 1964 (in press).

BRADY, J. V. Psychophysiology of emotional behavior. In A. J. Bachrach (Ed.) *Experimental foundations of clinical psychology.* New York: Basic, 1962.

ELLIS, N. R., BARNETT, C. D., & PRYER, M. W. Operant behavior in mental defectives: Exploratory studies. *J. exp. Anal. Behav.*, 1960, *3*, 63–69.

FERSTER, C. B. The use of the free operant in the analysis of behavior. *Psychol. Bull.*, 1953, *50*, 264–274.

LINDSLEY, O. R. Characteristics of the behavior of chronic psychotics as revealed by free-operant conditioning methods. *Dis. Nerv. Syst,* (Monograph Supplement), 1960, *21*, 66–78.

OLDS, J., & MILNER, P. Positive reinforcement produced by electrical stimulation of septal area and other regions of rat brain. *J. comp. physiol. Psychol.*, 1954, *47*, 419–427.

SIDMAN, M. Verplanck's analysis of Skinner. *Contemp. Psychol.*, 1956, *1*, 7–8.

SIDMAN, M. *Tactics of scientific research: evaluating experimental data in psychology.* New York: Basic, 1960.

SKINNER, B. F. *The behavior of organisms: an experimental analysis.* New York: Appleton, 1938.

SKINNER, B. F. Some contributions of an experimental analysis of behavior to psychology as a whole. *Amer. Psychologist*, 1953, *8*, 69–78.

STRUPP, H. Patient-doctor relationships: psychotherapist in the therapeutic process. In A. J. Bachrach (Ed.) *Experimental foundations of clinical psychology.* New York: Basic, 1962.

THOMPSON, D. A schema of response probability as a function of stimulus events. *Technical Report, ONR, Contract Nonr* 474 (8), University of Virginia, 1962.

WOLPE, J. *Psychotherapy by reciprocal inhibition.* Stanford: Stanford U. Press, 1958.

DISCUSSION

Question: If operant conditioning were used, how could you ever discover something like schizokinesis, which involves a split between an observable behavior and an internal physiological process?

Bachrach: I think that it has only been in recent years that physiological monitoring and behavioral correlates have taken on any real meaning. I think that Hefferline and his group at Columbia, for example, have made some significant contributions to the understanding of so-called unconscious behavior. This is because they have had adequate physiological monitoring. In any approach to physiology we insist that the covert must be rendered overt. You cannot talk about anxiety as a psychophysiological response unless, at the moment, you are able to monitor it. And I think that we are getting the techniques.

Let me talk very briefly about what Hefferline did. He had an electrode hooked up to the thumb of the subject, and an annoying, aversive hum or white noise was piped into the ear phones. The subject could terminate this if he gave a very minute thumb twitch, which could be monitored and amplified by EMG techniques. They found that this was subject to exactly the same laws of conditioning as were other types of behavior, that as in avoidance conditioning the subject could either escape the noise by a tiny muscle twitch or he could avoid the onset of the noise by this twitch. The interesting thing about this—and it relates to unconscious behavior—is that he had another group which he instructed to make a tiny muscle twitch which would terminate the noise if it came on, or would avoid the onset of the noise. And he found that none of the people in this latter group could deliberately and voluntarily make a twitch that was small enough. Now this is involuntary unconscious behavior, but the point I'm making is that it was rendered observable.

Now, what we are concerned about in operant conditioning, just as classical conditioners are, is the development of laws of behavior. We are not eliminating or overlooking the physiological. What we are asking is can we observe, can we report, can we record, and can we manipulate these events? And I think that there is enough evidence now to suggest that we may be able to do a great deal more than we could a few years ago.

Gantt: Several years ago I asked Professor Skinner, "What do you feel would be the changes in the cardiovascular system with conditioning?" He answered that he didn't think there would be any change. I asked him the same question this past February, and he said, "Furthermore, I have absolutely no interest in what happens with the cardiovascular system."

I don't think anybody would question the genius of Professor Skinner in what he has done with operant conditioning, but as you point out, and as Skinner has said quite openly, he is not interested in what goes on inside. Now I find Skinner refreshing, and think that perhaps he is making a contribution even in his emphasis on neglecting theory. Of course, he doesn't really neglect all theory, because if you get beyond the animal-training stage to practical training and education you have to have some theory to go on.

I think that the two systems, so-called classical conditioning and operant conditioning, contribute different things. They are different in their purposes. I have done some operant conditioning, too, and I don't feel that there is any difference in the underlying mechanism. I think the difference is in the experimenter. What are you going to look at? The person who does more of the Pavlovian type of conditioning tries to postulate, and, of course, he is treading on somewhat treacherous grounds when he makes postulates and hypotheses and theories. But at least he is trying to find out what is in back of these actions.

Now, as Dr. Bachrach has shown, and as all of Skinner's pupils in this country have given evidence, a great deal of progress can be made by neglecting almost entirely, but not completely, what goes on in the black box. Sometimes, though, I think you have to have a look at what goes on inside the black box, and I would like to ask Dr. Bachrach if he thinks that we should always neglect that, or should we neglect that only in this particular stage of the investigation of behavior.

Bachrach: I think that this point and one that most of the operant conditioners would share, is that we should not rush into unclear physiologizing. The "conceptual nervous system" involves concepts of irradiation, and so on, that have no specific neural correlates. I think that so much of the work on the reticular formation today is just of this character. Don Lindsley, one of the more excellent physiological psychologists, recognizes this when he refers jocularly to the reticular formation as the "reticular porridge," because it is so lumpy and ill-defined.

I don't think Skinner really has any objection to physiology, but rather to prematurely using physiological explanations or physiological processes to account for behavior. I think that Skinner is worried about the rush to physiological explanations. I think that he feels that the reticular formation is almost as inadequate as the id, the superego, and the ego as an explanatory concept. It is not that physiology is not fundamental, it's just that we have to be very, very careful of this prematurity. As we well know, many explanations have cropped up in the last ten or fifteen years on brain functioning, which have turned out to be inadequate or inaccurate.

Question: How do you explain unconscious mental phenomena?

Bachrach: I must confess that "unconscious mental" processes is a concept that I don't even bother with. I think that the whole concept of mentalistic phenomena is something which is beyond scientific investigation at present. When we can render these things observable, then I think we can study them. This does not throw out the realities of thinking and remembering and forgetting, but I merely say that they are not currently subject to study in terms of what we have got.

Another thing. I am always concerned by the perpetuation of some of these mentalistic approaches in introductory textbooks of psychology. For example, you will have one chapter called, "Central Nervous System Activity," and another chapter called "Thinking." I always thought thinking was part of the central nervous system activity, and this perpetuation of dualism is certainly unwarranted in science. I believe that behaviorism as a methodology in the study of behavior or psychological phenomena has to follow the same monistic principle as any other science.

II

Critical Comments
on the
Psychoanalytic Zeitgeist

INTRODUCTION

William Parson, M.D.

It is a pleasure to welcome the very distinguished physician and scientist, Dr. Percival Bailey of Chicago. When I was a medical student, some twenty-five years ago, Dr. Bailey's book on tumors of the brain (Bailey, 1933) was the standard textbook. In preparation for introducing him I went around to talk to my friends in neurosurgery and neuropathology, and I said, "What's a good book?" Said they, "We still use Bailey's book." And it seemed to me that this was a very interesting thing, and a challenge, perhaps, to any of you who like to write psychiatric textbooks, and perhaps a little bit of an insight into the nature of the problem we are dealing with here.

With respect to Dr. Bailey's career, I have taken the liberty of chatting with him with the idea in mind that I might share with you a few of the anecdotes that I gleaned from him. He didn't seem too troubled about it, so I will tell you that he trained in psychiatry very early, and after he had this training, he wrote two letters, one to Harvey Cushing and another to Adolf Meyer. Now there's a lot in this story if you get the essence of it. The essence is that Harvey Cushing answered by return mail, and Adolf Meyer took three months to reply. I hope you psychiatrists get the essence of that story, because what was the gain of neurosurgery, neuropathology, neuroanatomy, and neurophysiology was to some extent, I would suppose, the delay in the advancement of psychiatric thinking. In any event, Dr. Bailey did go to Boston and spent a number of years with Dr. Cushing and established the great tumor registry there. Dr. Bailey spent some time abroad, and worked in psychiatry intermittently through this. His interest has always been in the mind—or the brain—or the nervous system—wherever you would like to use those terms to orient yourself. Then he got the call, as we say in the academic world, to come back to Chicago as professor of neurosurgery, and he worked at the University of Chicago for a while in this field.

Then, about ten years ago, he went back into the field of psychiatry, and is currently director of research for the Illinois State Psychiatric Institute. Now, some of you perhaps know that he has written some very provocative articles. He tells me that he had literally thousands of letters, many of them, shall I say, upset letters, or letters from upset people, after his address before the American Psychiatric Association (Bailey, 1956). And if he had any left, he would still be sending reprints of his provocative article in *Perspectives in Biology* (1961), which some of you may have read and most others of you would be interested to read.

What sort of man is this? Well, I went back to his textbook on brain tumors and I found two things that are interesting. One is for you who think a little bit like the analysts, and that is grist for your mill: he dedicated his book to his mother, and his wife, and his teacher, who is also a lady. Now this, to me, is rather an attractive thing. Use it as you will. The other thing is that he quoted in his book a statement by Foster Kennedy, a very keen, gifted neurologist who died a few years ago. The quotation reads, "he who cares . . . must bring to his problem much thought and stout action. There is need also for a formidable optimism, for the dice of the gods are loaded."

REFERENCES

BAILEY, P. *Intracranial tumors.* Springfield: Charles C Thomas, 1933.
BAILEY, P. The great psychiatric revolution. *Amer. J. Psychiat.,* 1956, *113,* 387–406.
BAILEY, P. A rigged radio interview—with illustrations of various ego-ideals. *Perspect. Biol. Med.,* 1961, *4,* 199–265.

SIGMUND FREUD:

SCIENTIFIC PERIOD (1873–1897)

Percival Bailey, M.D.

> . . . biographers are fixated on their heroes in quite a special way. . . . They thus present us with what is in fact a cold, strange, ideal figure. . . . That they should do this is regrettable. . . . It does not detract from his greatness . . . if we bring together the factors which have stamped him with the tragic mark of failure.
>
> S. FREUD.

This conference is overshadowed by two men who have exerted powerful influence on our times—Sigmund Freud and Ivan Petrovich Pavlov. I shall spend my time on an important period of the life and works of Freud, leaving Pavlov to others who are more familiar with him. I have been reproached for using *ad hominem* arguments in my discussions of the work of Freud. It is obvious that the truth of a proposition cannot be proven by arguing from the character of the proposer, but the development of any body of knowledge (*Wissenschaft*) cannot be understood without an intimate knowledge of the lives of the men who created it. Freud wrote, "None of my works has been so completely my own as this [dream interpretation]; it is my own dung heap, my own seedling and a *nova species mihi*." This is also the opinion of Freud's devoted disciple and biographer, Ernest Jones, who wrote in his preface (Jones, 1953–1957),* "Psychoanalysis . . . can be profitably studied only as an historical

---

* The monumental biography of Freud by Jones has been a major source of the factual material in this paper.

evolution, never as a perfected body of knowledge, and its development was peculiarly and intimately bound up with the personality of its founder." No one would deny that the founder of psychoanalysis was Sigmund Freud, although Ernest Jones is largely responsible for its success as a world movement.

Sigmund Freud was born in Freiberg, Moravia, on May 6, 1856. His father was a wool merchant whose business was ruined by the inflation following the restoration of 1851. When Sigmund was three years old the family left Freiberg and, after wandering around, finally settled in Vienna in 1860, and Sigmund grew up in that urbane atmosphere. His father was a man of liberal views who did not observe the traditional orthodox customs, but spent much time reading the Talmud and had great respect for the traditional wisdom of the Jewish people. The young Freud was not taken to the synagogue, although, when he was small, he often went to the Catholic cathedral with the Czech maid.

The scientific secular atmosphere had reached Vienna and during his school days was permeating the intellectual world. This Freud recognized, and tried to fit himself into that atmosphere, although strictness and accuracy were alien to his nature; in school he liked literature and history but showed no interest in science and was poor in mathematics. He liked phantasy and identified himself with such Semitic heroes as Hannibal and Massena, one of Napoleon's marshals who was supposed to be Jewish. Under the influence of a friend, he thought he might study law, but later shifted to medicine.

He would have been an excellent lawyer, but became instead a reluctant physician against the advice of his father, who knew that he could not abide the sight of blood. This is the way Freud accounted for his decision—at least this is one of many variants:

> Although we lived in very limited circumstances, my father insisted that in my choice I should follow my own inclinations. Neither at that time, nor indeed in my later life, did I feel any particular predilection for the career of a physician. I was moved, rather, by a sort of curiosity, which was, however, directed more towards *human concerns* rather than towards natural objects; nor had I grasped the importance of observation as one of the best means of gratifying it. My early familiarity with the Bible story at a time almost before I had learned the art of reading had, as I recognized much later, an enduring effect upon the direction of my interest. Under the powerful influence of a school friendship with a boy rather my senior who grew up to be a well-known politician I developed a wish to study law like him and to engage in social activities. At the same time, the theories of Darwin which were then of topical interest, strangely attracted me, for they

held out hopes of an extraordinary advance in our understanding of the world; and it was hearing Goethe's beautiful essay on Nature read aloud at a popular lecture by Professor Carl Brühl just before I left school that decided me to become a medical student.

It is prophetic of the later Freud that he could be so inspired by a "pantheistic paean to the glories of nature." It could not possibly have inspired him to a scientific career. "There is an eternal life, a coming into being and a movement in her; and yet she goes not forward. She is always changing and there is never a moment when she is at rest. Of staying she has no notion and upon inaction she has laid her curse, etc. etc. etc." Freud's statement can be understood only to mean that he saw in medicine a chance to study nature.

So in October 1873, Freud matriculated in the medical school of the university and tried seriously, for the next quarter of a century, to make a scientist of himself, with how little success will be evident as we proceed. His entry into medicine coincided with a severe financial crash in which his father's small capital was lost. Nevertheless, the whole family scrimped and physically hungered to put him through medical school, while Freud dallied over his medical studies and finally took eight years to complete them, undoubtedly because he wanted to become a scientist and had a great distaste for the practice of medicine. He seems not to have been too distressed by the privations of the family, having been accustomed to consider himself its most important member. He irritably terminated his sister's musical interests, bought more books than he could afford, borrowed money right and left, and generally absorbed the resources of the family.

Later he was to write that he now ruthlessly suppressed his tendency to metaphysical speculation. At least he tried. During the first year, in addition to anatomy, botany, chemistry, microscopy, and mineralogy, he followed only two extracurricular courses, one on biology and Darwinism and another on the physiology of voice and speech. The second year, however, found him following the reading seminar in philosophy of Brentano, although it was no longer obligatory for medical students. This seminar he followed assiduously for three years and took other courses with Brentano on Aristotle's Logic. But he also began to make attempts to cultivate biology. He began to work in practical zoology in the laboratory of the zoologist Claus, head of the Institute of Comparative Anatomy. In March 1876, Freud was sent for a few weeks to the Zoological Experimental Station at Trieste, where he studied the gonadic structure of the eel. Freud was put to the task of checking the findings of Syrski, who, in 1874, had described a small lobed organ which he believed represented the testes not theretofore identified in the eel. In all, Freud dissected some 400 eels and found the Syrski organ in many of them. On microscopical examination, however, he could not prove that it was a testis. It was over this work that Jones first remarks one of Freud's distinguishing characteristics—the tendency to blame his failures on someone else. In the abstract of his scientific writings which he presented to the university some twenty years later there is easily detected a note of resentment toward the teacher who suggested this study. This personal feeling broke out again when Freud wrote, in 1925: "During my first three years at the university I was compelled to make the discovery that the peculiarities and limitations of my life denied me all success in many departments of science into which my youthful eagerness had plunged me. At length in Ernst Brücke's laboratory I found rest and satisfaction." Now follows the backhanded thrust at his former teacher, Claus: "and men, too, whom I could respect and take as my models."

Brücke was now the embodiment of his ideal—Science with a capital "S." He was an excellent example of the disciplined scientist that Freud now desired to become. Freud remained in his institute for six years from that autumn of 1876. Brücke, probably because of Freud's previous training with Claus, put him at the modest task of trying to determine the nature of the Reissner cells in *Petromyzon*. It is characteristic that Freud went at this problem with the microscope alone, making no attempt to attack it experimentally, although he was working in a physiological laboratory where the two assistants, Exner and Fleischl, made extensive use of the experimental method, and he certainly must have known that Brücke, his chief, had become famous by studies on the structure of cells which combined both methods. If Freud had shown any inclination to use the experimental method, Brücke would surely have encouraged him. Not only was Brücke not averse to it; he preferred students to present their own projects for research. But there was in Freud's nature, as Jones remarks, something passive which kept him, for most of his life, sitting and listening. Nevertheless, he later reproached the professedly revered Brücke for condemning him to a subordinate part of physiology.

However that may be, Freud soon came to Brücke and announced that he had discovered that nonmyelinated fibers of the posterior roots originated in some of the Reissner cells. Later, after Brücke had presented the finding to the Academy of Sciences on January 4, 1877, Freud wrote in a second report that he had found similar information in a paper by Kutschin published as early as 1863. He wrote: "Only shortly after the publication of my paper did I find . . . an abstract of a paper by Kutschin which contains important information on the origin of the posterior root. . . . I can only say that Kutschin's statements—

perhaps because his pictures were not available to the German histologists—were quite generally overlooked."

Freud continued to work along these lines, extending his studies to the nerve cells of the crayfish, improved the method of fixation of nervous tissue, developed a method of impregnating nerve fibers with gold chloride. In the summer of 1879 he worked for a while in the laboratory of Professor Stricker, who reported that, at his suggestion, Freud had worked for six months at some experiments on acinous glands but accomplished nothing. Six years later he returned to Stricker's laboratory and worked at some experiments on the functions of glands in relation to the circulatory system, but accomplished nothing again, and never after attempted the experimental method except for an abortive and amateurish effort with Koller to test the effect of cocaine on muscular strength.

Meanwhile Freud was following his medical studies and finally took his M.D. degree on March 31, 1881. But he went straight on working in Brücke's laboratory, simultaneously trying his hand at chemistry in the laboratory of Ludwig, in spite of the fact that his family was impoverished and was being supported partly by contributions of relatives; while Freud himself was subsisting on loans from friends, teachers, and relatives. Also, he had become engaged. Brücke, who had been content to have him work in the laboratory as a student, now pointed out to him how unrealistic was his conduct and advised him to enter actively into the practice of medicine.

In later years, characteristically, he placed the blame on anti-Semitism. Stefan Zweig remarks how Freud exaggerated the anti-Semitism of Vienna, the most urbane of the great capitals of Europe. Actually, he had shown no particular aptitude for scientific investigation. His conduct was dictated not only by the dream of becoming a famous scientist, but also by an intense distaste for the practice of medicine. Now he harbored a deep-seated resentment against Brücke for his failure, as he had against Claus, despite his alleged reverence for Brücke.

So at long last, on July 31, 1882, he inscribed himself in the General Hospital of Vienna. Beginning with Nothnagel, on May 1, 1883, he transferred soon to Meynert's Psychiatric Clinic, where he remained for five months, his main purely psychiatric experience. Nothnagel and Meynert were of great assistance to him later. When he applied on January 2, 1885, for the rank of privatdozent in neuropathology, it was Brücke, Nothnagel, and Meynert who were the committee of the faculty who examined him and reported on his work. In this year he also applied for and obtained a traveling grant, left the General Hospital on August 31, 1885, and went to Paris and Charcot's clinic at the Salpêtrière. He could now present himself as privatdozent in neuropathology.

In the meanwhile had occurred another of the characteristic attempts of Freud to shift the blame for failure on to someone else, this time his fiancée. Freud had obtained from Merck some cocaine, which he had tried on himself and others, taking it internally or by injection. He had been reading about the Indian tribes in Peru who chewed coca leaves to increase their capacity to work and endure fatigue. This gave him the idea to try it for nervous exhaustion, being himself troubled with neurasthenia. He found that the drug gave him a sense of well-being without robbing him of energy for work. He also gave the drug to his friend Fleischl, who was addicted to morphine. He sent some to his fiancée, he gave it to his sisters, his friends, and his patients. It became a miracle drug to him on which he now pinned his hopes for fame and fortune. He wrote a dithyrambic essay on the drug which was published in the *Centralblatt für die gesammte Therapie*. He looked on cocaine as an analgesic and energizer.

The usefulness of the drug as a local anesthetic was discovered by his friend Koller. Koller tried it on the eyes of animals and established its use as an ophthalmological anesthetic. Koller reported his experiments to the Ophthalmological Congress in Heidelberg, while Freud was on a visit to his fiancée. When, later on, it became obvious that all Freud's other hopes for the drug were in vain, and that its effect as a local anesthetic was its only permanent usefulness, Freud was bitterly disappointed. Moreover, he had made his friend Fleischl an addict to the drug; which he attributed to the fact that he had administered it by hypodermic needle. He blamed missing its use as a local anesthetic on his fiancée. In his account he begins, "I may here go back a little and explain how it was the fault of my fiancée that I was not already famous at that early age" and he ends, "Koller is therefore rightly regarded as the discoverer of local anesthesia by cocaine, which became so important in minor surgery; but I bore my fiancée no grudge for the interruption of my work." As Jones remarks, "The rather unnecessary initial and concluding remarks suggest that someone should be blamed."

While Freud was doing his stint in Meynert's clinic he obtained permission to work in the laboratory as well, for Meynert was a distinguished anatomist. Freud concentrated during the next two years on the medulla oblongata, making use of Flechsig's suggestion to use the fetal brain, in which only part of the pathways were myelinated. He published three papers on this work; the first was concerned with roots and connections of the acoustic nerve; the second, with the inferior peduncle of the cerebellum; and the third dealt with the fifth, eighth, ninth, and tenth nerves. These were routine, careful studies, well within Freud's tastes and possibilities.

Freud remained in Paris, in the clinic of Charcot, from October 13,

1885, to February 28, 1886. He tried to continue his anatomical studies in the laboratory of the Salpêtrière, but found conditions there unsatisfactory and considered leaving after only two months. But he changed his mind and became happy once again when the idea occurred to him to translate Charcot's lessons into German. Charcot thereupon invited Freud to his home a few times, where he overheard some remarks which he later used in his sexual theories. Freud was also very much impressed by Charcot's account of how he proceeded to make his discoveries by looking long and hard at the data until they arranged themselves in some order in his mind. Brücke would have seen immediately that this is only the first step in making a scientific discovery, but Brücke was now rejected and Charcot had become Freud's current oracle. Besides, this account appealed to the passivity of Freud's nature. He was never again to progress beyond this first step, and he was not long enough or intimately enough involved in the clinic of the Salpêtrière to learn, as I did years later, how the internes manufactured the data for Charcot. The story has recently been published by Guillain. Freud was to fall into the same trap, only he manufactured his own data, as we shall see.

On returning to Vienna, Freud was placed by Kassowitz on the staff of the Institute for Children's Diseases, where he worked for many years, using the material for studies of palsies in children. Notable were his two excellent monographs, one on central diplegias which was warmly praised by Pierre Marie, and another, in collaboration with Oscar Rie, on cerebral hemiplegia. Freud also published, in 1891, a book on aphasia, in which he criticized the doctrine that various aphasias could be explained by subcortical lesions, and adopted the functional explanation of Bastian that radiation of the derangement from the damaged areas was involved. This book is an excellent example of his speculative tendencies, but he never followed it up with confirmatory data. His work on cerebral palsies, however, he followed with a comprehensive monograph entitled "Infantile Cerebral Palsies" in Nothnagel's Encyclopedia, in 1897. This ended his neurological period. It was the last he was to write on neurological topics.

Up to this time Freud had shown himself to be a competent anatomist but an incompetent experimentalist. He had made himself an authority on the clinical manifestations of cerebral palsies, and had written a thoughtful speculative review of aphasia. All in all, as Jones says, "There was little to foretell the existence of a genius."

We turn now to another theme in which we see him led into a colossal blunder. Freud was always very secretive about his sexual life, but there are numerous indications that he was greatly preoccupied by what Jones calls the "control of his animal nature." For example, he speaks often of his neurasthenia in his letters to Fliess, and in elaborating his neurotica, made masturbation its essential cause. His long engagement (June 17,

1882, to September 13, 1886) may have exacerbated his own troubles. But he made up for lost time after marriage: the sixth child was born on December 3, 1895. We know that his sexual life ended shortly thereafter, probably the result of a profound depression. By this time he had begun to suspect his scientific blunder, to worry about his professional future, and to suffer from a very considerable psychoneurosis. In 1894 Breuer had already begun to dissociate himself from Freud's exaggerations of the sexual factor in the etiology of neuroses. Nevertheless, Freud read a long discussion of the etiology of hysteria to the Doktor Kollegium in Vienna, taking up three evenings (October 14, 21, 28, 1895), in which he maintained that "in men an anxiety neurosis is rooted in abstinence, in women it occurs mostly through coitus interruptus and that every hysteria is founded in repression, always with a sexual content." The last he had heard from Charcot, and the statement fitted his own preoccupations: Freud always judged the truth of any suggestion by himself. That these lectures were well received must have encouraged him.

On May 2, 1896, Freud gave an address to the Society of Psychiatry and Neurology in Vienna in which he presented his parental seduction theory. He maintained, on the basis of the analysis of thirteen cases, that the cause of hysteria is a passive sexual experience before puberty, specifically a traumatic seduction. On this supposed discovery Freud had again pinned all his hopes for fame and fortune. He said that he believed he had made a discovery in neuropathology comparable to the discovery of the source of the Nile. But he was not now talking to a lot of general practitioners. He was talking to an elite group which heard him with astonished disapproval. The chairman, Krafft-Ebing, certainly not one to be shocked by a discussion of sex, remarked dryly, "It sounds like a scientific fairy tale." Freud was crushed and never again addressed the society. Nevertheless, on September 21, 1897, in a letter to Fliess he admitted that he had made a far-reaching blunder. This is the way he put it: "Let me tell you straight away the great secret which has been slowly dawning on me in recent months. I no longer believe in my neurotica." Eight long years were to pass before he publicly retracted the seduction theory of neuroses, and then only after he had been able to persuade himself that, in the interpretation of dreams, he had found a more reliable method of penetrating the unconscious. This time there was no one to whom he could shift the blame. In his chagrin and depression he joined B'nai B'rith, seeking refuge in the Jewish community and in the Jewish mystical tradition, so that what he subsequently wrote smacked clearly of the cabbala.

In his autobiography he tells the story thus:

Under the pressure of the technical procedure which I used at the time, the majority of my patients reproduced from their childhood scenes in which they were sexually seduced by some grown-up person. . . . I believed these stories, and consequently supposed that I had discovered the roots of the subsequent neurosis in these experiences of sexual seduction in childhood . . . when, however, I was at last obliged to recognize that these scenes of seduction had never taken place, and that they were only phantasies which my patients had made up or which I myself had perhaps forced upon them, I was for some time completely at a loss. My confidence alike in my technique and in its results suffered a severe blow.

Nevertheless, he continued to use the method in spite of his doubts. In his *Analysis of a Phobia in a Five-Year-Old-Boy,* first published in 1909, he wrote: "It is true that during the analysis Hans had to be told many things that he could not say himself, that he had to be presented with thoughts which he had so far shown no signs of possessing. . . . This detracts from the evidential value of the analysis; but the procedure is the same in every case." Concerning the dubious value of patients' reports as scientific data one might also cite Jones (II, 429): "With a patient he [Freud] was treating before the war, whose life history I knew intimately, I would come across instance after instance when he was believing statements which I knew to be certainly untrue."

Freud could never admit that he had really made a mistake. As he himself said, after he had thought for a while in a certain pattern he could no longer think otherwise. He was soon to write, "Analysis had led by the right paths back to these sexual traumas, and yet they were not true." So he continued to use free association, only depending now on his own free associations as more dependable, and generalizing from his own associations, he clung to the sexual etiology of neuroses, merely pushing the roots back into infancy. And psychoanalysis has continued to build on the unverified, and usually unverifiable, verbal reports by patients of past events which may never have taken place, as Freud found to his sorrow.

He seems not to have realized that a dream is even less satisfactory as scientific data than the results of free association. The latter can sometimes be checked by contemporary documents or the statements of witnesses, but there is no way of checking a dream. For several years I circulated among psychoanalysts, attending their banquets and parties and listening to their talk. On more than one occasion I have heard an analyst recount a dream several times in the course of a day, improving it on each occasion. Neurotic patients (also some analysts) are disciples of Mark Twain, who said that one should not spoil a good story by telling the exact truth. I remember also the statement of Otto Rank that whenever he threatened to stop treatment his patients began to give him the sort of dreams in which he was interested. Freud and numerous disciples have built successful practices on the interpretation of dreams, but have built no science on them.

During those years Freud, while suffering from a "considerable psychoneurosis," to quote Jones, undertook to search his own unconscious and to analyze his own dreams. He also began to construct a new theory on the basis of an examination of himself, a procedure of dubious scientific value. But he was desperate now. His critics had been proven right and his hopes of world renown were gone. Worse than that, his practice had diminished and he had a growing family to feed. No wonder that he searched desperately to find within himself the roots of his errors and a new orientation. It was no longer possible for him to do scientific work, for which, by his own admission, he was not fitted, so he plunged with abandon into speculation based on what he found in his own psyche, a procedure which Jones would have us believe Freud was the first human being to employ.

Freud's subsequent writings contain numerous statements which indicate that he knew what he was doing:

> There is nothing for it but to summon help from the Witch—the Witch metapsychology. Without metaphysical speculation and theorizing—I had almost said phantasy—we shall not get a step further. Unfortunately, here as elsewhere, what our Witch reveals is neither very clear nor very exact.

> This insight sounds plausible, but it is in the first place too uncertain and lets in the second place more new questions and doubts emerge than we can answer.

> I can say that I have made many beginnings and thrown out many suggestions. Something may come of them in the future: But I cannot myself tell whether it will be much or little.

Naturally, Freud hoped that some of his speculations might turn out to be true, but it is not our task to follow all the interesting sophistries by means of which he deluded himself and his followers into believing that he had been correct after all, so that today he is practically deified by them. For an excellent example of his ability along these lines, read the first of his introductory lectures on psychoanalysis after he was made a professorial lecturer. Suffice it for us to realize that this was a very serious scientific blunder indeed, and leave his disciples to believe that, as Ernest Jones writes, this failure was his greatest triumph. We sense here the influence of the Christian tradition working in Jones's un-conscious. One sees vaguely in the background the figure of Christ on the Cross. To Freud, who read extensively during this period in the literature of mysticism and demonology, it must have seemed more like selling his soul to the Devil in return for a livelihood for his family and surcease from his obsessive self-scrutiny.

Even if one could agree with Jones: "His claim to greatness, indeed, lies largely in his honesty and courage with which he struggled and over-came his own inner difficulties and emotional conflicts by means which have been of inestimable value to others," and admired the stoical courage with which he faced not only his emotional difficulties but also his physical ones, one would not be obliged to acclaim him a great scientist. As he wrote to his friend Fliess, "I am not really a man of sci-ence, not an observer, not an experimenter and not a thinker. I am noth-ing but by temperament a conquistador. . . ." And again to Marie Bonaparte, "I have very restricted capacities, or talents, none at all for the natural sciences, nothing for mathematics, nothing for anything quantita-tive."

With the publication of *The Interpretation of Dreams,* Freud threw science to the winds, and gave himself over wholeheartedly to his primary love—speculation [*The Witch,* he called it, after Goethe] and spent the rest of his life in guessing, as he said, how the mind was put together, or, as he said on another occasion, in building an artificial structure of hy-potheses. This he sometimes called a *Wissenschaft.* Although Freud was a master of the German language, he often wrote somewhat carelessly. He repeatedly used the word "Wissenschaft" without further specification. In German the word "Wissenschaft" means a body of knowledge or teaching. But there are many kinds of *Wissenschaften,* such as *Naturwis-senschaft* (natural science) and *Geisteswissenschaft* (say, mind-soul science).

Ruesch places psychoanalysis among the *Geisteswissenschaften.* Freud himself called it a *Geistesrichtung*—an orientation of the spirit. That its method is not a scientific method, in the strict sense of the term, Freud knew very well. "For a psychoanalysis is really not an impartial scientific investigation, but a therapeutic measure." (*Eine Psychoanalyse ist eben keine tendenzlose, wissenschaftliche Untersuchung, sondern ein thera-peutischer Eingriff.*) In this passage, it is obvious that by *wissenschaftliche* Freud meant the method by which our knowledge of natural science has been built up. Psychoanalysis is certainly not a "natural science" (*Naturwissenschaft*). Its followers, however, try desperately to make it appear so, because of the prestige our society attaches to "science."

As Jones said, 1897 was the acme of Freud's life, for it was then that he began to liberate himself from the restraint of the scientific method for which, by his own admission and that of his biographer and devoted disciple, Ernest Jones, he had no aptitude. He was now free to speculate concerning the problems of life and death which, as he wrote, assailed him in the morning and robbed him of his composure and his spirits. Jones (I, 268) identified these problems as the nature of man, the relationship of mind to body, and how man came to be a self-conscious animal, or, in another place, the nature of man, the existence of God, and the aim of life. These speculations he called metapsychology. Freud's thought was dominantly humanistic, not scientific.

At one time Freud tried to outline a scientific psychology. The manuscript of that attempt, which he called *The Project,* has been published. He abandoned this project because there was insufficient scientific data available at the time about the higher nervous functions. Today, with the development of communication theory and the theory of conditioning, we are in a much better position to make such a synthesis. It is interesting and significant that, faced by this impasse, the true character of Freud became apparent and he launched into visionary speculation, whereas Pavlov plunged into the experimental laboratory and laid the foundations of a true *Naturwissenschaft.*

REFERENCES

BAKAN, D. *Sigmund Freud and the Jewish mystical tradition.* Princeton: Van Nostrand, 1958.

FREUD, S. *The origins of psycho-analysis.* Marie Bonaparte, Anna Freud, & E. Kris (Eds.). New York: Basic, 1954.

FREUD, S. *An autobiographical study.* London: Hogarth, 1954.

GUILLAIN, G. J. M. *Charcot, 1825–1893, his life—his work.* (Transl. Pearce Bailey). New York: Harper, 1959.

JONES, E. *The life and work of Sigmund Freud.* 3 vols. New York: Basic, 1953–1957.

JONES, E. *Free associations: Memories of a psycho-analyst.* New York: Basic, 1959.

DISCUSSION

Question: Do you consider that any of Freud's findings are valuable?

Bailey: I said that he made many speculations. That's what he said himself. Some of these speculations might turn out to be worthwhile, and many of them might not. Today there is a great deal of discussion going on in scientific circles concerning the value of many of the suggestions which he made. The trouble is that many of them are expressed in such ill-defined terms that they cannot be subjected to experimental tests.

Question: One of the most widely accepted of Freud's contributions is his discovery of the unconscious. Surely there are internal events of which we are not conscious? Yet you imply that Freud's hypothesis of the unconscious mind has not been proved.

Bailey: Events of which we are unconscious are a somatic matter. There are certainly all sorts of things that go on in the central nervous system, including the brain. There are unconscious processes going on in the brain, and if you want to call them "the unconscious," I have no objection. But there is no scientific proof of the existence of a functional system corresponding to the "dynamic unconscious" postulated by Freud.

Parsons: Dr. Stevenson, would you care to make a comment?

Stevenson: It seems to me that the contribution of Freud and psychoanalysis was not so much in the specific concepts or doctrines or findings, as in drawing attention to the plasticity of human personality, and I think we owe a lot to the psychoanalytic movement for combating the excessive nineteenth-century emphasis on organic brain disease as the origin of mental disorder, and for stressing the role of personal experiences in the etiology of mental disorders. I think that is one important contribution. Secondly, I think the contribution of Freud and psychoanalysts regarding the influence of early experiences in human personality and mental disorders is an extremely important one.

Bailey: I would broadly agree with what you have said, but I would add that the psychoanalysts were not the only ones to discover the relevance of personal experience. At the same time as Freud was working, Pierre Janet also became aware of this and had much influence in propagating the idea in many quarters. Later on, Freud tried to discredit Janet. In regard to the other matter, the importance of the early period for the development of neuroses, the psychoanalysts did not discover that either. Among others, the Jesuits knew it for centuries, before the psychoanalysts ever appeared on the scene.

Question: Why did you stop at 1897 in Freud's career?

Bailey: I thought I had made that quite clear, but if you will accept the term science in the sense of *Naturwissenschaft,* or *natural* science, Freud didn't do any more "natural scientific" research after 1897. He ended there. After that what he did was speculate. He never tried to subject any of his ideas to experimental tests, and furthermore, he was quite hostile to the suggestion that they be subjected to experimental tests. He maintained that they were self-evident and did not need any demonstration. So I stopped at 1897 because that was the last time that he wrote a scientific paper in the sense of *Naturwissenschaft.*

SOME REFLECTIONS ON PSYCHOANALYSIS, HYPNOSIS, AND FAITH HEALING

Corbett H. Thigpen, M.D.
and
Hervey M. Cleckley, M.D.

Conditioned reflex therapy (Salter, 1949) and treatment by reciprocal inhibition (Wolpe, 1958) have not been extensively applied in the United States. They have been used for a number of years in England and encouraging reports of their results have been published (Eysenck, 1960).

It is true that a case for the conditioning therapies should not be built on the ashes of another method. The foundations of the Freudian theory in particular are, it seems to us, composed of little more than paper and would hardly make a suitable foundation for anything of value. If the conditioning therapies have validity, they will rise and stand firmly on their own demonstrated results. Not infrequently psychiatrists have said that if one is to criticize the present dynamic school of psychiatry (based mainly on Freudian principles), then one should have something to offer as an alternative. Despite the promising reports that have appeared, the conditioning therapies may eventually prove to be of little value. They are, however, something to consider as alternatives to the Freudian method.

Unlike dianetics, Christian Science, Zen Buddhism, phrenology, the healing practices of Oral Roberts, and various other faiths or schools of scientism, Freudian theory is a dominating influence today in American psychiatry. For this reason it concerns us all. This theory also seems to hold great appeal for emotionally disturbed or overcredulous creators of popular art and literature. From them sometimes emerge bizarre drama and painting, and unrealistically perverted novels, confidently based on concepts attributed to Freud and assumed to be supported by science

(Cleckley, 1957; Sievers, 1955). Though few would probably dare maintain that scientific principles can be applied today in psychiatry as accurately as in physics, it is nevertheless important that we strive to base our work on these principles and methods in so far as they are available and applicable. It is perhaps even more important that we accurately recognize these methods and not confuse them with what may have little or no relation to them. Our first responsibility as physicians is to do what we can to restore the patient to health, or, if this is beyond us, at least to give him what relief we can. It is then also our responsibility to ask ourselves, from time to time, if there is evidence that indicates whether or not what we are doing is achieving these results.

Psychoanalysis has been in use for well over fifty years. During the last decade modifications of it, or methods based upon it (dynamic psychotherapy, psychoanalytically oriented psychotherapy, and so on) have become increasingly popular in this country. These methods have been applied to scores of thousands of patients: to the psychotic, to the delinquent, to the criminal, and, most extensively of all, to the psychoneurotic. The reader of our current psychiatric literature cannot fail to see that our most influential spokesmen regard them as the established methods of choice for dealing with most, if not all, psychiatric disorders. The logical conclusion from this would be to assume that such therapy must be remarkably effective in its results (Thigpen, 1960).

It would also be logical to suppose that during this period of more than half a century convincing evidence from numerous statistical studies would be available to demonstrate this assumed effectiveness. Several studies have been reported in which results are compared between groups treated over long periods by psychoanalysis and other groups who were treated briefly by relatively simple measures available to the physician practicing general medicine. The statistics do not indicate an appreciable difference between the results in the two groups (Cheney and Landis, 1935; Landis, 1937; Salter, 1952). Nor does either group included in these studies show a better percentage of recovery and improvement than groups who have had no treatment at all. It is perhaps not fair to conclude from the available data that psychoanalysis and the other forms of psychotherapy have been proved worthless. There are, however, no statistical studies that could support a claim for their efficacy. Such claims must, let us frankly admit, be made not on evidence but on faith (Eysenck, 1953).

Many who maintain that Freud made genuine and profoundly significant discoveries credit him with revealing things that have been wellknown for centuries. Long before Freud was born, as Altschule (1957) so clearly shows, it was widely recognized that man is often motivated in thought and in behavior by impulses he does not recognize or admit.

Even such truisms as the fact that influences in early life tend to shape the development of a personality are sometimes claimed as new and monumental discoveries by Freud. In a critical examination of Freudian theory it is not such points as these that demand questioning.

Let us instead examine the concepts that *originated* with Freud and still serve as the foundation of the popular psychodynamic creed. Among these is the assumption that every little boy specifically desires intercourse with his mother (the Oedipal situation) and that because of these desires he fears that his father will punish him by castration (castration fear). It is also maintained that Freud has proved beyond question that every little girl thinks that she was born with a penis but that this penis has been cut off in a mutilating punishment. Can we really accept the confident claim that she longs for the lost penis and turns desperately to her father in the hope that he may be able to repair this tragic loss? When she is disappointed in this forlorn hope, so it is devoutly said, the little girl then wants the father's penis. Foiled again, does she then decide that she wants him to give her a baby? So the theory insists.

Let us look also at Freud's "discovery" that every living man and woman on earth has homosexual desires that throughout life vigorously compete with normal biologic sexual aims. Many of the astonishing pronouncements that Freud makes regarding the so-called oral and anal phases of development also tax ordinary credulity and deserve examination. These claims are made on the basis of mere assumption and analogy. Must one, on this basis alone, reverently believe that during a bowel movement little boys suffer terrible fears of genital mutilation because the anal sphincter severs an elongated and rounded mass of feces? Shall we then go farther with the creed and say that the trauma of these boys is mitigated by their realizing that within them they have material to produce more "brown penises" (Baruch, 1952)?

Let us also consider soberly the scientific method of a learned Freudian psychiatrist as he interprets the popularity of attractive young girls who parade in scanty and charming costumes at football games. The drum majorette stands out in front of the band. The male genital organ (especially when in erection) stands out in front of the body as a whole. From this the psychiatrist, boldly and "dynamically," leaps to the confident conclusion that men who look on eagerly are not interested by what they are well aware of seeing in the voluptuous young lady but, instead, are driven by impulses toward fellatio or sodomy which she arouses in the unconscious, where she represents not the naturally enticing attributes of the female but a penis in erection (Grotjahn, 1957). It cannot be denied that he is accurately applying the method by which Freud came to his own basic conclusions.

Does development of so-called insight through the acceptance of such beliefs as these, after innumerable hours of therapy, really cure or ameliorate any mental illness that the patient might have? Indeed, if he genuinely does come to believe even the items just mentioned, would it not be more reasonable to conclude that he has developed a morbid confusion rather than valuable insight?

Such claims as these invite questions. Along with others, we have in the past posed a number of questions to those who insist that such psychoanalytic assumptions are correct (Thigpen, 1960). These questions were posed in the hope of obtaining answers that would contain some support for the assumptions. It also occurred to us that if evidence cannot be offered, it would then seem that the questions might serve as a stimulus for a large and influential body of psychiatrists to re-examine their conclusions.

It has proved most difficult to obtain any answers that are pertinent or that squarely meet the points that have been raised. The responses so far elicited fall into one or another of these categories:

1. The questions are coolly ignored. Do the analysts and others who subscribe to these psychodynamics believe that all who question will tire and go away? Do they assume that the questions will eventually be forgotten?

2. A sarcastic or supercilious retort is aroused which is often a personal comment on the ignorance (or perhaps the "resistance") of the questioner.

3. Ancient truisms are promptly and confidently flourished. Though many of these have been popular maxims for centuries (for example, that early environmental influence may affect the development of the child) they are nevertheless piously ascribed to Freud as stupendous discoveries.

4. These truisms are complacently and arbitrarily mixed with unfounded speculations, and the oddly compounded ingredients are then presented under a single term. It is apparently assumed that if any item in this mixed package is accepted, then the truth of all the rest is thereby established.

5. Some who answer resort to a naïve use of analogy, as if analogy itself constituted evidence. Illustrating by analogy is one thing; proving a point by analogy is quite another. Many children in grammar school are well aware of this distinction.

6. Others, in attempting an answer, redefine simple (or complex) terms to fit the theory. Curiously enough, many seem to feel that this affords confirmation of the theory. For example, if no true sexual in-

terest can be demonstrated when one man on a bus offers another man a cigarette, the definition of "sex" is extended to include all interest that one person can feel for another. Q.E.D.: All people are bisexual. This unwarranted but convenient extension of the accepted meaning of the word "sexual" does not, however, constitute a discovery of homosexual drives in the unconscious. (For a more detailed discussion of these points see Cleckley [1957].)

7. Polysyllabic neologisms are devised to replace well-defined and generally accepted terms for familiar things, and sometimes to indicate imaginary abstractions based on pure assumption. This often engenders a false impression of high technical knowledge, as when one solemnly (and sometimes pompously) speaks of a young man as oedipally fixated and ambivalently attempting a libidinal cathexis with a heterosexual love-object of anal character who has become a mother-surrogate through (unconscious) identification with the maternal imago. This language lends itself readily to the construction of verbal artifacts (resounding terms without demonstrable referents) which can be glibly assumed to exist in the unconscious, and then manipulated freely to furnish specious evidence for almost any imaginable theory, sane or insane (Korzybski, 1941).

8. Some who reply fall back on the familiar Freudian dogma that no one is capable of judging the validity of the theory until he has been successfully analyzed. Since no one is classified as having completed his analysis until he has accepted the theory, apparently only those in agreement are regarded as competent to comment.

9. Some answers show deep faith in a practice long familiar in Freudian reasoning. This practice is to formulate a hypothesis, and then, as time passes and discussion progresses, to regard the original hypothesis with ever-increasing confidence. Eventually it is accepted as a fact, and recognized by the elect as a sound basis on which to establish still another assumption.

10. This practice of "proving" a point by offering as evidence other points previously assumed often leads to a growth not only of considerable velocity at the onset, but soon, also, to an acceleration that suggests geometrical progression.

Recently some who adhere strongly to Freudian theory have become more vigorous in deprecating those who question it. Lack of faith is even said to be "antipsychiatric." It is sometimes implied that the skeptic is indifferent to the plight of the mentally ill and is a serious obstacle to those who strive to help them. It has been said that criticism of the popular theory may impede the efforts of those who are calling for many more millions from the government for "mental hygiene projects." Some years ago a letter to the editor was printed in *The American Journal of Psychiatry* bitterly criticizing him for allowing articles that challenge the analytic creed to be published (*Am. Jour. Psychiat.*, 1956).

In view of this it is surprising to find that some of the more academic Freudians, faced with their apparent lack of therapeutic success, are now openly saying that psychoanalysis was not primarily intended to treat patients, and should therefore not be judged on its efficacy (or lack of efficacy) in relieving them. They quote Freud in support of this claim. They maintain that the value of the method really lies in its investigational prowess. Much ado has been made about this type of research, and vast sums of federal money are spent upon it—to what purpose one can still only speculate. How will this defense of the method impress practicing analysts whose chief efforts are devoted to the treatment of patients? Is the House of Freud again dividing against itself?

Those who express skepticism about the Freudian theories are often told to leave well enough alone unless they have something better to offer. Some who make these protests seem to ignore the crucial importance of trying to find out, even at this late hour, whether or not they have been building a pseudo-science upon a fallacy. To find that one has been doing this would indeed be painful. But to be doing it and persistently refuse to realize it would eventually be calamitous. The speed and confidence with which one is driving down the wrong road can scarcely be regarded as the measure of progress toward one's destination.[1]

At a symposium held in 1958 by the New York University Institute of Philosophy many interesting points about analytic theory and method were discussed. Participating in this were "some of the world's leading psychoanalysts and outstanding philosophers of science." Some of the analysts present were Heinz Hartmann, Lawrence Kubie, Abram Kardiner, and Jacob Arlow. The discussions at the symposium were published in a volume edited by Sidney Hook (Hook, 1959). A few comments by philosophers of science follow:

> But on the Freudian theory itself, as a body of doctrine for which factual validity can be reasonably claimed, I can only echo the Scottish verdict: Not proven.—Ernest Nagel, John Dewey Professor of Philosophy, Columbia University.
>
> It [psychoanalysis] must lay down its arms because the monistic dogma of psychoanalysis is palpably inadequate to account not only

---

[1] A collection of eleven essays by various authors critical of the psychoanalytic position has recently been edited by Rachman (1963).

for the varied achievements of creative artists and philosophers and scientists but also for the work of poetic mythologists like Freud himself.—Sidney Hook, Professor of Philosophy, New York University.

Unless psychoanalysis has better clinical or experimental successes than alternative theories, it can hardly aspire to scientific status. —Sidney Hook.

. . . how in the name of Roger Bacon could a psychoanalyst imagine that his own hopelessly contaminated, uncontrolled, unfollowed-up, unvalidated, unformalized estimation of success has ever established a single cure as being his own work? —Michael Scriven, Department of Philosophy, Swarthmore College.

Freudian doctrine . . . provides a language for saying silly things in an impressive way. . . . Freudian language offers a way of inflating the importance of findings that are merely banal. —Charles Frankel, Professor of Philosophy, Columbia University.

When the data seem to be inconsistent with the theory, then they get reinterpreted so as to be consistent with it. A theory which explains everything, which cannot be contradicted by any sort of facts, does not deserve to be called a scientific theory. —Raphael Demos, Professor of Philosophy, Harvard University.

The opinion is submitted by us that the method used by Freud and his followers to "prove" their theories is a travesty of scientific method. Such methods, sometimes called scientism, often produce in the unwary, and in those emotionally committed to the methods, an illusion that they are actually engaged in fruitful scientific work.

One of the great dangers to psychiatry today rests in the fact that many who are devoutly convinced that Freudian theory has been scientifically established and proved beyond question have obtained high teaching posts and other positions of authority. Thus the Freudian theory is propounded as scientific gospel to the vulnerable, while other, and more modest, schools of psychological thought are ignored. By such means has the Freudian theory tyrannized American psychiatry. Those who express doubt of it are sometimes treated as heretics who would impede the progress of salvation.

Psychotherapy in some form or another has been applied by various schools of psychiatry. Many good things have been claimed at this conference for the conditioning therapies. It seems appropriate to inquire a little more deeply into the nature of psychotherapy and to pose some questions about conditioning and other therapies.

Let us first consider a method familiar for approximately two centuries and, when successfully applied, the most vividly demonstrable and probably the most effective psychologic measure ever devised by man. This, of course, is hypnosis. Since the 1840's, major surgical procedures have been carried out under hypnosis (Allen, 1937; Mason, 1955; Esdaile, 1957; Kroger and De Lee, 1957). Legs have been amputated and laparotomies performed on patients who have denied that any pain was experienced and who showed no signs even of discomfort. Today reports are still accumulating of successful and complete anesthesia in surgery and in childbirth, and of the relief of excruciating pain in severe burns and in malignancy (Crasilneck, 1955, 1956; Dorcus, 1948). It is difficult to doubt that these things have been done repeatedly and are being done frequently today. What then, we ask ourselves, is hypnosis? And how does it achieve its results?

Perhaps these questions cannot be adequately answered. Let us, however, consider a few points brought out by Barber, who has published impressive studies on hypnosis during recent years:

> A series of experiments . . . indicate that appropriately predisposed persons do not need an "hypnotic induction" and need not appear to be in "the trance state" to carry out the typical behaviors which have been associated with the word "hypnosis" (Barber, 1961).

> The good hypnotic subject . . . (a) has favorable attitudes toward hypnosis, (b) is strongly motivated to be hypnotized and (c) expects to be hypnotized (Barber, 1960).

> The subject must possess the attitude of "basic trust" toward oneself and others (Barber, 1960).

> The phenomena of hypnosis can be explained by one general principle: the behavior of the hypnotic subject is a direct function of his altered perception of himself and of the situation. . . . He is ready, willing and expecting—he is "set"—to perceive the operator's statements as valid descriptions of what is or is not occurring (Barber, 1957).

> In hypnosis the subject behaves in "unusual" ways only when the interacting and overlapping processes between the subject and the hypnotist are effective in altering the subject's "perception" and interpretations of himself and his surroundings (Barber, 1958b).

> The hypnotist attempts to "guide" the subject to conclude that the suggestions are literally true statements (Barber, 1958a).

Barber emphasizes the importance of faith in the induction of hypnosis. He also points out that a trance state is not necessary to bring out, in some subjects, impressive manifestations of hypnosis. Is it not

likely that patients who undergo major surgical operation without pain
have somehow come to believe literally that what the hypnotist tells them
is true? And that, however unreasonable it may be, it is absolutely and
unquestionably true? The hypnotist's statement, like the word of God,
has become infallible and proof against any contradiction. Not even that
fearful contradiction of the senses that ordinarily would arise from the
surgeon's knife can prevail against this faith-induced conviction. By
means we little understand this invincible faith successfully blocks from
awareness the dire bombardment of neural impulses that would otherwise
constitute unbearable agony.

In connection with hypnosis let us consider other impressive manifestations that have occurred in various forms through the centuries and
that can be readily demonstrated today all over the world. These, like the
results of hypnosis, often appear to be dependent on an unusual interpersonal relation and on a specific faith that is profound. Some of these
manifestations consist of an intense and scarcely explicable abreaction of
emotion that to an uninvolved observer may appear to be hysterical or
even psychotic. Scores of examples of such behavior were presented by
William James long ago in his *Varieties of Religious Experience* (1902).
William Sargant in his remarkably impressive book has commented very
pertinently on many others (1961).

Sometimes these explosive emotional reactions begin with great distress, and progress through ecstasy to deep peace and tranquillity. Sometimes, but by no means always, they are followed by permanent changes
in attitude and behavior. The reactions of many to John Wesley's preaching, the transports of modern cultists who handle poisonous snakes during religious rites, groups who become worked up to emotional frenzies
during protracted sessions of rock and roll dancing, as well as the
multitudes who during the fourteenth century fell into psychotically
aberrant behavior known as the dancing mania—all demonstrate the effects
of a force that Sargant discusses at length and cogently. As he points out,
this force can be evoked by various means and in widely different settings.

Those who handle rattlesnakes during a revival meeting say that it is
the power of God that transforms them in the conversion that sometimes
occurs. Those who develop a trancelike state of euphoria to the protracted beat of rock and roll are usually not pursuing religious aims. The
patient who undergoes a painless laparotomy under hypnosis is tranquil
and motionless in his responses to the hypnotist's quiet voice. During the
dancing mania those hundreds who continued their bacchantic leaps,
"screaming and foaming with fury" hour after hour, were described as
becoming "insensible to external impressions." During their "roaring and
foaming" progress they apparently became no less invulnerable to pain

than the hypnotized patient during his operation. Some continued until they fell dead from injuries and exhaustion. Others, after collapsing, slowly regained their strength and, emerging from the frenzy, returned soberly to their work and other responsibilities.

By quotations from John Wesley and from Grinker and Spiegel, Sargant illustrates vivid similarities between the emotional (and physiological) manifestations evoked by Wesley's preaching in 1739 and those shown during abreaction of war experiences by patients given barbiturate drugs by the two psychiatrists in 1942. Sargant makes this comment: "Wesley and his followers attributed the phenomenon to the intervention of the Holy Ghost. . . . Grinker and Spiegel, on the other hand, believed that their results demonstrated the correctness of Freud's theories in which they . . . themselves believed" (Sargant, 1961).

Most analytically oriented forms of psychotherapy demand many hours of association between the patient and the psychiatrist, sometimes hundreds of hours. The patient, in revealing his most intimate feelings and freely discussing his personal affairs, develops profound and complicated emotional relations with the learned man in whom, it is likely to seem, lies his only hope of relief.

As Barber has pointed out, hypnotic control (or something very similar to it) may occur in several other ways besides a sudden and dramatic induction into the familiar trance state. He also makes it clear that hypnosis in its less obvious and typical applications can indeed exert powerful influence upon the subject. Though the analytically oriented psychotherapist seeks to avoid exerting overt hypnotic influence upon his patient, it is difficult to see how some of the basic factors involved in hypnosis can be avoided. In ordinary hypnosis they are openly and quickly demonstrated, and are often spectacularly flourished. In prolonged psychotherapy such factors are certainly less overt. But who can say they do not operate insidiously, concealed behind the ostensible framework or the elaborate theoretical structuring of the program, whether or not they are consciously recognized by the patient or by the therapist? It has been said that only a very wise hypnotist can be certain as to who is being hypnotized during the imperfectly understood process that occurs between the practitioner and his subject.

The more closely we examine a number of these human reactions, not readily explicable in rational terms, the more plainly it appears that an essential factor in all, or at least most, of them is the achievement of profound and irrationally induced faith. Perhaps we do not at once discern the operations of faith in the trancelike euphoria achieved by fanatical devotees of rock and roll. Yet through these dancers' progressive response to reiterations of the beat, there emerges a peculiar emotional surrender, sometimes with a release of intense feelings that definitely suggests abreaction or conversion. It is not difficult to see here also a similarity to what occurs with the incantations, the corybantic dancing and the rhythmic tom-tom beating that, during voodoo rites, facilitate the attainment of mystic dedication to Erszulie or other pagan deities. During the voodoo rites there is sometimes induced a faith so invincible that it is hailed as literal possession by the god or goddess (Sargant, 1961). Even during the less primitive rituals of rock and roll, along with the milder ecstasies and furors that have often shaken adolescent crowds in the presence of Elvis Presley, there is likely to occur also an infatuated commitment to the idol himself, a reason-eclipsing and cabalistic dedication that could not be attained without the operation of this obscurely engendered faith.

Is it not possible that all psychotherapy may be, perhaps to a considerable degree, literally faith healing? This is not necessarily a criticism of psychotherapy, or of hypnosis; for if faith, either in man or in God, will help the mentally ill, should we not respectfully welcome it? Should we not also, if this is true, seek to recognize more clearly what we have been doing and apply this important factor more effectively and more wisely?

When impressive changes occur during prolonged psychotherapy several questions arise. Are these a result of the therapist's rational application of valid and abstruse knowledge of the human personality to the patient's problem? Or do these changes occur chiefly through a profound faith that the patient develops in the therapist, and which acts in ways we understand no more completely than we understand what occurs during hypnosis or during the many impressive manifestations described by Sargant?

In the therapy of reciprocal inhibition, deep muscle relaxation is strongly encouraged. Muscular relaxation is also one of the first steps in hypnosis. Many believe that a patient who is in a state of deep muscular relaxation is in the first phase of hypnosis. In reciprocal inhibition therapy this muscular relaxation is apparently carried into as deep a degree of hypnosis as the patient and the therapist are capable of eliciting. If Barber's observations are true—that the patient, in greater or lesser degree (depending on depth of trance), believes that what the hypnotist says is valid—then we wonder if the recoveries reported by Wolpe and his followers might not, to some degree at least, be attributable to this intense and complex interpersonal situation. Is it not possible that the apparent effect of Pavlovian principles, to which Wolpe attributes his recoveries, may not be due, at least in part, to other causes? The points we suggest deserve critical examination. Careful evaluation of them may eventually lead us to a more substantial basis for psychotherapy. If we learn that we are working chiefly through the imperfectly understood but powerful effects of faith, let us admit it to be so, use it with more insight, and seek better and more straightforward means of application.

It will be interesting to see whether or not the therapies based on Pavlov's work will prove regularly effective. The investigations of Wolpe and Salter encourage one to hope that they will. It would be proper, however, to abandon the Pavlovian principles if evidence of their efficacy is not available within the next fifty years.

REFERENCES

ALLEN, C. *Modern discoveries in medical psychology.* London: Macmillan, 1937.

ALTSCHULE, M. D. *Roots of modern psychiatry.* New York: Grune & Stratton, 1957.

AMERICAN JOURNAL OF PSYCHIATRY. Correspondence. 1956, *113,* 466–469.

BARBER, T. X. Hypnosis as perceptual-cognitive restructuring: III. From somnambulism to auto-hypnosis. *J. Psychol.,* 1957, *44,* 299–304.

BARBER, T. X. Hypnosis as perceptual-cognitive restructuring: IV. Negative hallucinations. *J. Psychol.,* 1958, *46,* 187–201 (a).

BARBER, T. X. The concept of "hypnosis." *J. Psychol.,* 1958, *45,* 115–131 (b).

BARBER, T. X. The necessary and sufficient conditions for hypnotic behavior. *Amer. J. clin. Hypnosis,* 1960, *3,* 31–42.

BARBER, T. X. Physiological effects of hypnosis. *Psychol. Bull.,* 1961, *58,* 390–419.

BARUCH, D. W. *One little boy.* New York: Julian Press, 1952.

CHENEY, C. O., & LANDIS, C. A program for the determination of the therapeutic effectiveness of psychoanalytic method. *Amer. J. Psychiat.,* 1935, *91,* 1161–1165.

CLECKLEY, H. *The caricature of love.* New York: Ronald, 1957.

CRASILNECK, H. B., STIRMAN, J. A., WILSON, B. J., MCCRANIE, E. J., & FOGELMAN, M. J. The use of hypnosis in the management of the patient with burns. *J. Amer. med. Ass.,* 1955, *158,* 103–106.

CRASILNECK, H. B., MCCRANIE, E. J., & JENKINS, M. T. Special indications for hypnosis as a method of anesthesia. *J. Amer. med. Ass.,* 1956, *162,* 1606–1608.

DORCUS, R. M., & KIRKNER, F. J. The use of hypnosis in the suppression of intractable pain. *J. Abnorm. Soc. Psychol.,* 1948, *43,* 237–239.

ESDAILE, J. *Hypnosis in medicine and surgery.* New York: Julian Press, 1957.

EYSENCK, H. J. *The uses and abuses of psychology.* London: Penguin, 1953.

EYSENCK, H. J. *Behaviour therapy and the neuroses.* London: Pergamon, 1960.

GROTJAHN, M. *Beyond laughter.* New York: McGraw-Hill, 1957.

HOOK, S. *Psychoanalysis, scientific method and philosophy.* New York: New York U. Press, 1959.

JAMES, W. *Varieties of religious experience.* New York: Modern Library (copyright 1902).

KORZYBSKI, A. *Science and sanity* (ed. 2). Lancaster, Pa.: Science Press, 1941.

KROGER, W. S., & DE LEE, S. T. The use of hypnoanesthesia for caesarean section and hysterectomy. *J. Amer. med. Ass.*, 1957, *163*, 422–424.

LANDIS, C. Chapter V in L. E. Hinsie (Ed.) *Concepts of psychotherapy.* New York: Columbia U. Press, 1937.

MASON, A. A. Surgery under hypnosis. *Anaesthesia*, 1955, *10*, 295–299.

RACHMAN, S. *Critical essays on psychoanalysis.* New York: Pergamon, 1963.

SALTER, A. *Conditioned reflex therapy.* New York: Farrar, Straus, 1949. Capricorn Books—Putnam's Sons, 1961.

SALTER, A. *The case against psychoanalysis.* New York: Holt, Rinehart and Winston, 1952; Citadel, 1963.

SARGANT, W. *Battle for the mind.* Baltimore: Penguin, 1961.

SIEVERS, W. D. *Freud on Broadway.* New York: Hermitage House, 1955.

THIGPEN, C. H. Multiple personality. *The New Physician*, 1960, *9*, 27–33.

WOLPE, J. *Psychotherapy by reciprocal inhibition.* Stanford: Stanford U. Press, 1958.

DISCUSSION

Wolpe: Dr. Thigpen has raised the question whether reciprocal inhibition methods in particular and conditioning methods in general are effective. I have already said that as far as the evidence has gone, they seem to be effective, and it has been impressive that in many cases obvious change occurs in a very short time. Furthermore, in certain cases that we have employed as experimental study cases, we have been able to demonstrate that change takes place only in association with those circumstances in which theory would predict change, even though the patient has no way of knowing what the therapist predicts (Wolpe, 1962). Now, Dr. Thigpen made the statement that reciprocal inhibition methods lean heavily on hypnosis. This is not so. Hypnosis is used only in one technique, desensitization, and it is not always used in that. Relaxation, which Dr. Thigpen is prepared to equate with hypnosis, is indeed a constant feature of desensitization; but the equation is a most dubious one, and Jacobson (1938) has strongly contested it. In any event, in most other conditioning techniques neither hypnosis nor relaxation is used. Now, there is a general question: how much of change depends upon "faith" in the therapist? If "faith" were all, change would occur under all conditions, and not only in the conditions our theory predicts.

Thigpen: Like Barber, I believe that some factors operating in psychotherapy are similar to those in hypnosis, even though they are less obvious. I believe the therapist can exert powerful influence by suggestion, without the ordinary hypnotic trance, and sometimes without suspecting that he is exerting such an influence. Dr. Wolpe is a highly dynamic (with apologies to the dynamicists) and forceful personality. That he avidly and devoutly believes in his method of treatment is without question. The "conditioning" process which he uses from one hour to thirty or more hours is likely to build up a feeling of confidence in the patient—confidence in Dr. Wolpe and his method of treatment. Dr. Wolpe is likewise utilizing other psychotherapeutic factors: he is frank in saying that he carefully inquires into the patient's past and tries to relate earlier experiences to his present illness. He attempts to promote the patient's self-assurance as well. Who can say that these factors may not foster faith in Dr. Wolpe and his techniques, perhaps a faith that plays a part in therapy that is as important as the Pavlovian techniques and Dr. Wolpe's theoretical beliefs?

Simple relaxation and closing of the eyes play an important part in hypnotic induction. Dr. Wolpe candidly says that if he can induce hypnosis he does so. The closer, I would think, that he can get a patient to hypnotic trance, the better and more rapid his therapeutic results might be. Though Jacobson may have questioned the influence of faith, as Dr. Wolpe says, has he produced evidence to rule this out?

I did not say that faith is the only factor involved. What I said is that I believe it to be the chief factor. Other factors likely to play a part are these: inducing changes in the patient's environment or persuading him to accept his situation; reassuring the patient; encouraging him to relate his past life in detail and to discuss the development of his present attitudes. Factors that do seem common to all schools of psychotherapy are: (1) encouraging the patient to discuss his problems at length; (2) permitting the passage of time to promote repair and healing; (3) fostering the patient's faith in the therapist's ability to help him. In psychoses, and many severe neuroses, beneficial changes often do not occur under any conditions. I am of the belief that beneficial changes do occur in all schools of psychotherapy, and not just under the conditions which the reciprocal inhibition theory predicts.

Dr. Wolpe says that "Change takes place only in association with those circumstances in which theory would predict it." This suggests that changes occur when they are expected. The factors which induce faith are still omnipresent. Even though the patient may have no way of knowing what the therapist predicts, it is obvious that the patient expects a change for the better by whatever type of therapy is employed. It is not necessary for the patient to understand the theory, or to know what the therapist expects, for beneficial changes to occur. A successful therapist, wittingly or unwittingly, exerts a profound influence on his patients by his personality.

Question: Surely the success of the therapy of experimental neuroses indicates that psychotherapy is a matter of conditioning?

Thigpen: This depends on what you mean by "conditioning." If by "conditioning" one means conditioning a patient to believe in the therapist and his method of treatment, yes. If you mean, however, conditioning as in reciprocal inhibition therapy, I do not know. I wonder if reciprocal inhibition therapy might induce an illusion in which both the therapist and the patient develop faith and through which they expect improvement. If reciprocal inhibition therapy and if other complex personality theories or theories of treatment are in the main illusory, how then, one might ask, can our modern psychotherapists bring about any help at all? We should not forget that an illusion may catalyze or open to awareness other things that are important and that are not illusions. Through a psychological theory, no matter how scientifically unsound, or absurd and superstitious, a person may develop an emotional change that will reveal to him something that is not necessarily dependent on that theory or assumption, but may indeed prove to be an eternal verity! Perhaps it may be a truth he desperately needed but would not have found except for the stepping stone of his faith, though the original faith was in something without basis in reality.

Please remember that I am not saying that conditioning therapy is without basis in fact. For all I know, every bit of it may be entirely factual. What I am saying is that it must be proven and that we cannot neglect this factor of faith.

Gantt: I would like to hear Dr. Thigpen elaborate just a little bit on the idea that Pavlovian science may not be applicable to the human being. Is it because you think that work on animals is not applicable, or do you think that the material that it deals with is not relevant to behavioral problems? The other thing is, when you speak of faith— faith is, of course, a very complex thing, and I think both of us could detect it when it is present, but we like in science to try to analyze these things and to see if there is any simpler element in it. Now I think a lot of faith is simply the conditioned effect of one individual on another. Do you feel that there is any way to analyze it? Would you feel that it is profitable to attack the concept or just to take it for granted as we take a great many concepts in everyday language—love, for example—so that it is often difficult for one person to know what another person means?

Thigpen: I certainly do not know that Pavlovian science may not be applicable to the human being. The Russians have apparently used this with success in brainwashing. Their tactics are on the classical Pavlovian hypothesis. It is interesting, however, that although a few succumbed to this negative conditioning, thousands upon thousands held firm and true to those things in which they had been trained or conditioned through life to believe. I do not know if purely Pavlovian principles without the interpersonal relationship which induces faith can be successfully applied in the treatment of mental sicknesses. Until this factor of faith is eliminated I do not see how we can properly judge whether the purely scientific Pavlovian principles are the sole or even the main determining factor.

The human being has an astonishingly complex cerebral cortex and an infinitely greater development and complexity of personality than any animal. He would, I think, be a far more difficult subject to condition in the Pavlovian sense than a monkey or a cat or mouse. That is not to say, however, that I maintain that man cannot be conditioned or reconditioned. I am sure that he can be, but I believe that there are limits. Man is essentially conditioned throughout his life to believe certain things in politics, religion, and other areas. I suspect that you are right in saying that faith is simply the conditioning effect of one person on another. But the conditioning that you are talking about is different even though it has much in common with the principles advocated in the conditioned reflex theory.

I suspect there are ways of analyzing faith. I am not inclined to attack the Pavlovian concept, but rather to learn more about faith and how much it influences the results obtained through conditioning therapy and other methods of psychotherapy.

I don't know offhand of experiments to determine this. This should be a job for an experimental scientist. I am a clinician. That does not mean, however, that I would not be interested in collaborating with a scientist who might wish to observe how I might influence a patient to improve or recover.

REFERENCES

JACOBSON, E. *Progressive relaxation.* Chicago: U. Chicago Press, 1938.
WOLPE, J. Isolation of a conditioning procedure as the crucial psychotherapeutic factor. *J. nerv. ment. Dis.,* 1962, *134,* 316–329.

III

Associated Experimental Data

AUTONOMIC CONDITIONING

W. Horsley Gantt, M.D.

There are, I believe, at the present time, only five people, besides myself, who worked with Pavlov and who are still working in the field. Four of these are in Russia—Asratyan, Kupalov, Vladimirova, and Anokhin— and Konorski is in Poland (Gantt, in Wortis, 1962a).

For a number of years the Pavlovian work was really neglected, and people were of the opinion, expressed to me by George Bernard Shaw, that every English bobby knows more about a dog than Pavlov (Pavlov, 1941). They got the idea that the conditional[1] reflex is that you ring a bell and you get a secretion of saliva. And that is about all there was to it. It is also of interest to see the prediction of H. G. Wells coming true to some extent. He wrote an article for the *New York Times* in the late 20's in which he excoriated George Bernard Shaw, saying that whereas Shaw's bombastic utterances would soon be forgotten after he was dead, Pavlov's work would grow in fame and would be even more important a hundred years after Pavlov's death than it was during his life (Gantt, 1962a). It is of interest to see this prediction on the way to being fulfilled.

Now we see that there is, I think, in this country, a healthy, growing interest in the Pavlovian work. Under the Stalin regime Russia had gone through an era in which the Russians had to look around to find a few approved people whose work they could endorse and follow, and they chose Pavlov as one of those. It was an era in Russia in which it was dangerous, even in the scientific field, to disagree with anything that Pavlov was supposed to have said. However, I understand now that

---

[1] Conditional (*ooslovny*) and not conditioned is Pavlov's original term.

there is much more free criticism in Russia, and that this era is fortunately over. Pavlov, of course, would never have endorsed such a point of view because he welcomed—as every real scientist does—criticism, really constructive criticism, and he felt that if his results could not stand up under criticism they were no good, and that criticism, therefore, was very helpful.

As you know, the conditional reflex was initiated with the study of the autonomic system. It was by observations of the gastric secretion and the salivary secretion, mainly at first with the gastric secretion, that Pavlov came upon the idea of the conditional reflex. In spite of this, if you mention to people in medicine any new organ whose functions are shown to be adaptable, to have this function of making new adaptations during the life of the individual, which is the conditional reflex, the specialists in that field will deny it. They are not accustomed to thinking that way. I have talked to a number of urologists who immediately reject the idea that there can be a conditional urinary secretion, that the kidney can secrete on a conditional reflex basis, although they may be familiar with the fact of salivary conditioning.

Now, because of this strong tradition in medicine, there is still a great need for demonstrating the conditional reflex in the various departments of medicine, a field which has hardly been touched at the present time. Pavlov's work with the conditional reflex went a long way to establish what Claude Bernard had tried to establish half a century before: determinism in biology—that it was possible to investigate biological phenomena by scientific methods. There had been many objections to this. Owing to the great complexity of the living organism, there was supposed to be some vital force which coordinated the various reactions and was responsible for the kind of integration that we see in the living organism.

There is a special difficulty when we begin to study the conditional reflex: the hazard of introducing subjective anthropomorphic explanations. This is understandable when you consider that if you study conditioning using the somatic musculature, the gross movements, that these are movements about which we are accustomed to have subjective feelings. We are acquainted with the various positions of the body. We are familiar with these movements and the feelings that go along with them, and we have been from early infancy. Therefore, we assume that we understand them, and that the feelings that go along with them (that you want this or that, or whatever feeling goes along with it) we then consider to be the explanation. The fallacy of this becomes apparent once you try to transfer this same kind of explanation to other organs, such as the liver or the stomach. Does the liver do what it does because it *wants* to do it—does it want to make glycogen or whatever it makes—does the stomach secrete a different composition of gastric juice to meat and to bread because it *wants* to do that? That would be accepted as the explanation of why your mouth waters; it's because you want food. Anyone can see the fallacy of this reasoning when he transfers these anthropomorphic explanations to organs whose activities we are not accustomed to knowing.

However, we have to remember that of the million things which go on within the living organism, we are conscious of only a very few. Yet all of these innumerable reactions, the internal secretions, the hundreds of chemical, biochemical interreactions that go on in this cell, the metabolic exchanges, we are absolutely unconscious of these, and we sit on the outside of them as much as we are on the outside of any phenomenon that we undertake to study, and it is only—not by introducing our subjective feelings—but by the scientific method, that we can begin to unravel some of these laws. But our task is Herculean. When we take up the study of what Pavlov called the higher nervous activity, the activity of the organism at the highest level, we have to admit, with great humility, that this is the most complex subject in the whole universe. Any living organism is a complex universe in itself, and the human being is the most complex of all the complexities that we know anything about in the universe. And so we have absolutely no insight into the workings of this organism, and we have to put together the laws by the same kind of studies that we use in analyzing and finding out the laws of any other physical phenomenon or of what occurs in lower organisms.

In regard to autonomic conditioning, I shall mention a few of the organs that Bykov worked with and conditioned when I was in Russia in the early 20's. Bykov was at that time conditioning urinary secretion. That work has been recently published in a wide-ranging book that has also been translated into English, but still the facts are not generally known or accepted (Bykov, 1957). Bykov has shown that the reactions of a number of other organs can be conditioned, viz., the thyroid endocrine secretions and even metabolic changes. Also there has been some work claiming that leucocytosis, immune body formation, can be a conditional reflex (Bykov, 1957). I mention these experiments, though I am not convinced that the work really proves this in regard to immune body reactions. My collaborators and I have studied a number of autonomic reactions besides the secretions of the salivary gland and of the stomach. We have worked with the vestibular reactions of balancing; we have devoted a number of years to the cardiac conditional reflexes.

We began this systematic investigation in 1939. We have also attempted to condition the sexual reflexes, and then we have made some study of a number of different drugs, using them either as an agent to produce a reaction to see if the effect can be conditioned, or to see what the influence of the drugs is on the conditional reflexes.

Since, as we know from its name, the conditional reflex is subject to the surrounding conditions, it is important, as Pavlov emphasized early in his work, to separate the animal from the surroundings, from disturbing influences in the environment and particularly from the people who worked with the animal. All the records—respiration, heart rate, blood pressure, movements, sexual erections—are made from outside the room and not in the presence of the animal.

We have conditioned a variety of animals in order to get a comparative view of the conditioning. It is very important that we use more than one animal, because animals vary a great deal in the specificity of their organs. The dog, for example, has a very responsive cardiovascular system, much more responsive than that of the human being, and is therefore a very useful animal for this particular kind of work. Penguins and other animals can form conditional reflexes quite readily. If you explore conditioning throughout the animal kingdom, you will find that practically all animals can be conditioned within a few trials, whether it be a worm or a higher animal. Dr. Liddell has been a pioneer in the comparative physiology of the conditional reflex. He has used a variety of animals—pig, goat, sheep, and dog. So if an animal can be conditioned at all, even a worm, it can be conditioned within a very few (five or six) trials.

In the recording of sexual reflexes, there is significant activity in respiration and the heart rate. In vestibular conditioning (Löwenbach, 1940) the dog is blindfolded, he has electrodes in the external ears, and a galvanic current is passed through the ears. As you know, it disturbs the vestibular mechanism for balancing, and the dog falls over. As he is blindfolded he cannot use his eyes for balancing. He has to depend on the vestibular system. However, if you precede the galvanic current which disturbs him, by some signal, then you can get him to fall over to the signal itself. This is of interest not only because you can get these vestibular reactions conditioned, but because it throws some light on the conditioning process.

There has been a good deal of discussion in psychology at various times as to whether or not the conditional reflex is a compensatory function. Under certain circumstances, it may be compensatory. However, I think those who work directly with the conditional reflex see that it is more likely to be a duplication of the unconditional reflex. If we were to reason from what we *think* should occur, we would think that the dog should take special means to balance himself when this signal comes which causes him to fall over. However, nature does not always work the way that we reason it should, or that we subjectively feel it should. The dog, instead of balancing himself to the signal, falls over.

The dog falls over completely. This falling is due not to the current through the ears; it is due to the bell which the dog has associated with the galvanic current. The falling over is purely a conditional reflex.

We have also been able to condition cerebellar reactions by putting electrodes within the nervous system. It is just as easy to condition the reaction when the stimulus is applied within the central nervous system as it is in the ordinary way. You do not need the peripheral structures in order to form the conditional reflex. By using induction coils and putting the electrodes in the cerebellum, you get certain ipsilateral movements that can be very easily conditioned, although we do not feel that there is necessarily any involvement of consciousness in this conditioning. The electrodes can be placed in various other locations, to substitute for the unconditional stimulus or for the conditional stimulus. In the latter case they may be inserted into the "silent" areas of the cortex, substituting for the bell or light, or whatever is used as a signal, or they can be applied to the posterior nerve roots or to the posterior columns. We see that the conditional reflex is primarily a centrally formed reaction, and that the periphery is not essential for the formation of the conditional reflex.

From the work of Bykov (1957) we know that the mechanism of the conditional reflex (for example, urinary secretion) can be either through the hormonal secretions or through the nerves. The pituitary is involved in the urinary conditional reflex as well as the nerves. The nerves can be eliminated and still there will be urinary conditioning, or you can eliminate the pituitary and get urinary conditioning, but if you both denervate the kidney and remove the hypophysis, then, according to the work of Bykov, it is not possible to form conditional reflexes.

When a dog is brought into the room, his heart rate may be 40 to 60. When he is listening to a tone, which elicits what Pavlov called the orienting reflex, turning around and paying attention to the sound, then the heart rate goes up; he also makes some movement (Gantt, 1952). Though the heart rate is not always proportional to the movement, it usually has a direct relationship. His movement is estimated on a scale of from 1 to 4. Where the movement is only 1+, the change in heart rate is the same. After about 140 repetitions of this tone, it is no longer novel, and there is no change in heart rate. We call this the extinction of the cardiac component of the orienting reflex. This dog is now ready to begin experiments forming the cardiac conditional reflex. His heart rate is now around 70, and all the time he is in the room it remains at a rather constant level. There is some difference observable when he is first brought in; when he is being stimulated, it is irregular.

When you give to the same dog a tone which has never been given in connection with anything in the laboratory life of the animal, after it has been repeated many times it causes no increase in heart rate, that is, the orienting reflex has been extinguished. When, for the first time, he is given a faradic shock after the tone, then the heart rate goes up to the faradic shock. Though the shock is given only once on this day, three things happen. The heart rate becomes irregular after that one stress situation, and the cardiac conditional reflex has been formed after that one reinforcement. The next time we give the tone, there is an increase in the heart rate to the tone. The usual thing is that we get the cardiac component of the conditional reflex formed after one coincidence, although the motor reaction and the salivary are not formed for some time afterward.

In the later stage in the formation of the cardiac conditional reflex in this dog, the one tone is given and always followed by shock. It is given for ten seconds and followed by shock. After two minutes— exactly two minutes—you give another tone, an octave higher, and you never shock the dog with this tone. Then, in another two minutes, after the inhibitory tone, you give the first reinforced tone. You will then see that the dog not only has differentiated, but the time reflex appears, an anticipatory reaction in the heart rate in the minute before he gets the tone. That is, the heart rate predicts when the signal is coming, if you train the dog in this precise way. He forms the *time reflex,* and the time reflex is evident much earlier in the cardiovascular system than it is in the motor reactions. As a later development, after about six months, the dog also shows some whining and some anticipatory reactions (Gantt, 1951; Gantt, 1957).

In another dog, with which Dr. Newton and some others have worked in the laboratory, Pedro (Pinto, 1957), the heart rate, after becoming accustomed to the camera, is around 40. When we begin to reinforce, you see the same thing that happened in the other dog. The first time that the faradic shock has been preceded by the signal, there is an increase in heart rate to the signal for the shock. There is no motor conditional reflex during this signal, although the cardiac conditional reflex is formed after one repetition.

In the same dog, on the next day, there is regularly an increase in heart rate to the tone. There is no motor conditional reflex during this time, and it does not appear until much later. There is a separation, then, between the functions—the visceral function, represented by the heart, and the motor function of the dog, lifting his foot to remove it from the plate where he gets the shock. If you were looking at this dog, as we used to do, without taking measurements of cardiac conditioning, if you were only observing his movements, you would say that he had not formed any conditional reflex, but by the study of the heart rate, you are able to see the conditional reflex appear after one conditioning event.

Dr. Newton (1961) has been doing some work showing that most of the dogs given only one reinforcement of the faradic shock form the cardiac conditional reflex, which continues even though you try to extinguish it. Though you do not repeat the faradic shock during the next two months these dogs continue to give the cardiac response. There is no motor response, but the cardiac response is extremely difficult to extinguish.

In another dog, Crazy, who was semidecorticated and with both *gyri cinguli* extirpated, during the first day of conditioning the dog formed a cardiac conditional reflex. There is no differentiation between the two signals, the one which is accompanied by the shock and the one which is not. After a few months this dog did form a perfect differentiation between the positive and the negative signals, showing that the cardiac conditional reflex is certainly not dependent upon the *gyrus cinguli*. There is retention of the cardiac conditional reflex after thirteen months in this dog.

After a normal dog had rested for thirteen months (Skipper, Dr. Gakenheimer's dog), his heart rate went up from about 90 to 130 when he was listening to the tone which had meant the shock; the heart rate went up only a few beats when he heard the other tone—the inhibitory one. On the same day, after this tone was reinforced, the change in heart rate to the positive and negative tones was parallel to the one on the same day before reinforcement, showing that there had been excellent retention during the thirteen months when the dog was not brought down for experimentation.

By the injection of bulbocapnine from outside the room (to avoid the effect of the presence of a person) by means of a tube in the jugular vein, catalepsy could be obtained. An auditory or visual signal preceded this injection, and an analogous cataleptic state appeared as a conditional reflex, as well as the EKG characteristic of bulbocapnine, viz., very tall T-waves (Perez-Cruet, Gantt, 1963).

I would like to point out several things. First, that any reaction of the body which is represented in the central nervous system can become a conditional reflex, but it must have a representation in the central nervous system. If you take a peripherally produced reaction by a drug, such as atropine on the heart rate, which occurs without involvement of the central nervous system, you cannot condition that increase in heart rate. Neither can you condition the change in heart rate to acetylcholine injection. But you can readily condition the change in heart rate to the *presence of a person*. Dr. Joseph Stephens did some work on that subject showing that if you sound a bell, the initial change in heart rate to the bell is that of an orienting reflex, an increase in heart rate. A person coming in at a separate time and petting the dog, rubbing him behind the ears, causes a decrease in heart rate, but if you give the bell ten seconds before you do the petting of the dog, and repeat that several times, then the bell will take on the quality of what the person is doing, and instead of increasing the heart rate, it will cause a decrease in the heart rate. My present collaborators (Drs. Royer, Newton, and others) and I are working on this subject, and we have found that the person can be a more powerful stimulus than the other stimuli that we are accustomed to use, such as food or even faradic shocks (Gantt, Newton, Stephens, 1960; Gantt, Newton, Royer, 1960). Often the person causes a bigger change in heart rate than any of the ordinary stimuli cause. Now this, I think, is a very important factor in therapy. It often seems to me that some specific result in therapy is referred to some other theory, when it really depends upon this general principle of the effect of one individual on another individual.

I also want to emphasize this difference between the formation of the cardiac conditional reflexes, the visceral conditional reflexes, and the more easily observable motor ones; that here we have a split between the functions of the organism so that the organism may be in adaptation with some of its organs and some of its reactions, but not with others. This phenomenon I term *schizokinesis* (Gantt, 1953; Gantt, 1960). Here we have a new view of the function of inhibition. Pavlov had thought that inhibition was a complete state, that when we extinguish the motor or salivary conditional reflex the dog will be in a more or less pure state of inhibition. From our study of the cardiovascular responses, we see that this may not be true at all; that the animal may be under very violent agitation from the visceral and emotional organs, even though he appears to be in adaptation with what we see on the surface.

There is another function which appears especially in the study of the visceral system's autonomic conditioning; and that is changes which occur within the nervous system, after a period of time, independently of the present environment, which I call *autokinesis* (Gantt, 1953; Gantt, 1960). There seems to be, certainly if you look at it from the point of view of function, in the animal this ability to change and, as far as we can determine, without any reference to the present external environment, but in relationship to what has occurred in the past. The animal, it seems, is capable of making his own internal adjustments. This subject is, at present, one which has not been explored. It is still largely a concept, but some neuroanatomical work has been done recently that lends some support to this.

Dr. Jerzy Rose, who was at Johns Hopkins, showed that there are new growths of nerve cells and nerve processes through one of the destroyed layers of the cortex. There has been some other recent work, from MIT, indicating that there is mitosis going on in the nervous elements in the brain, which would contradict the formerly held belief that new nerve cells cannot be formed in the adult mammal. So, from a study of the autonomic system, we are able to get not only a clearer and more delicate measure of its activity, but, by comparing the facts that we get from this study, we are enabled to see the existence of functions we have not seen before.

REFERENCES

BYKOV, K. M. *Cerebral cortex and internal organs.* (W. H. Gantt, Tr.) New York: Chemical Publishing Co., 1957.

GANTT, W. H. Comments on H. S. Liddell, Experimental induction of psychoneuroses by conditioned reflex with stress. In S. Cobb (Ed.) *Biology of mental health and disease.* New York: Harper, 1952.

GANTT, W. H. Principles of nervous breakdown—schizokinesis and autokinesis. *Ann. N.Y. Acad. Med.,* 1953, *56,* 143–163.

GANTT, W. H. Cardiovascular component of the conditional reflex to pain, food and other stimuli. *Physiol. Rev.,* 1960, *40* (Supp. 4), 266–291.

GANTT, W. H. Ivan Petrovich Pavlov. In J. Wortis (Ed.) *Recent advances in biological psychiatry* (Vol. IV). New York: Plenum, 1962 (a).

GANTT, W. H. Pavlov, champion of truth. *Mod. Med.,* 1962, *23,* 335–346 (b).

GANTT, W. H., & DYKMAN, R. A. Experimental psychogenic tachycardia. In P. Hoch & J. Zubin (Eds.) *Experimental psychopathology.* New York: Grune & Stratton, 1957.

GANTT, W. H., GAKENHEIMER, W. A., & STUNKARD, A. Development of cardiac reflex to time intervals. *Fed. Proc. Am. Physiol. Soc.,* 1951, *10,* 47–48.

GANTT, W. H., NEWTON, J. E. O., & ROYER, F. L. Development of the experimental neurosis: Mechanism and factors. *Proc. Third World Cong. Psychiat.,* 1960, Montreal, 991–995.

GANTT, W. H., NEWTON, J. E. O., & STEPHENS, J. Effect of person on conditional reflexes. *Psychosom. Med.,* 1960, *22,* 322–323.

GANTT, W. H., WISE, S. P., ROYER, F. L., NEWTON, J. E. O., & STEPHENS, J. Effect of "person" (experimenter) on cardiovascular functions. XXII Int. Congress of Physiol. Sciences, 1962, Leiden, Holland (Exhibit).

LÖWENBACH, H., & GANTT, W. H. Conditioned vestibular reactions. *J. Neurophysiol.,* 1940, *3,* 43–48.

NEWTON, J. E. O., ROYER, F. L., WHITMAN, J. R., & GANTT, W. H. One-trial cardiac conditioning in dogs. *Physiologist,* 1961, *4.*

PAVLOV, I. P. *Conditioned reflexes and psychiatry.* (W. H. Gantt, Tr.) New York: International, 1941.

PEREZ-CRUET, J., & GANTT, W. H. EKG T wave conditional reflexes to bulbocapnine. *Federat. Proc.,* 1963, *22,* 400.

PINTO, T., NEWTON, J. E. O., & GANTT, W. H. Comparative speed formation: Cardiovascular and motor conditioning. *Federat. Proc.,* 1957, *16.*

DISCUSSION

Question: How are these results applicable to human beings in the treatment situation?

Gantt: This is a very important and useful question, because it gives you an opportunity to justify scientific work. You can either take the position, "I am not interested in application. I am interested in *finding out.*" Or you can take the position, "What would have been the importance of Newtonian laws, at the time they were formulated, in flying an airplane?" Well, we know now that these laws were very important. So, I would say first, in general, that any relationship that you can find is of importance if it is really proven, and if it is a scientifically confirmed relationship; that the best we, as research scientists, can do is to establish laws. The people who are interested may apply them, as the therapists do. And then there is the other interest: finding out the relationships.

Now I can go on from that and say that I think that this concept does have applicability in medicine. Consider the question of hypertension, about which there is a great deal of discussion now, but we do not know all of its causes. We can produce hypertension in the laboratory dog; we can produce it by psychogenic means. Therefore, when we can produce something in a certain way, we know the cause. We have a certain power over the phenomenon when we know how it comes about, just as we know that tuberculosis is caused by the tubercle bacillus, as Koch proved. Then we have a certain ability to have some effect on tuberculosis, devoting our attention to the Koch bacillus. I think that, although I cannot give any direct rules now in regard to hypertension, we have at least a conceptual basis of some hypertension that begins on a psychogenic basis from stress. We see that these cardiac reactions, once they are formed, are very difficult to eradicate. We also see the influence of the individual, of the person, in producing the cardiac responses. All of this gives us an understanding and, of course, understanding is at the basis of the progress of medicine.

Question: Would you comment on the statement that "It's a long way from the cat to catatonia?"

Gantt: Well, that's a very nice phrase. We might as well ask, "Is there any importance to comparative physiology?" It's certainly true, some of the people, Andrew Salter here, and other people who deal primarily with the human being, certainly recognize that the human being is not a dog.

If we are studying cardiovascular reactions, there are marked advantages in using the dog as a subject. Last night I was talking with some people who had been trying to condition cardiac conditional reflexes in the human being. They stated that only one out of sixteen humans formed the cardiac conditional reflex to the faradic shock that they were using. Now this is a marked difference. The dog is very reactive. The human being is not nearly so reactive in this cardiovascular system. I have not worked with catatonia in cats. But we do get it in the dog.

Question: We have difficulty extinguishing the motor reflex to shock, even if there is an avoidance response to shock every time. But we can hardly keep the salivary reflex alive. As you know, it extinguishes with reinforcement, and we are struggling with this problem right now at the University of Georgia. So I would like to know what your ideas are about the difficulties in keeping the salivary reflex alive.

Gantt: The salivary reflex depends on the state of hunger in the animal. Dogs vary a great deal. I cannot answer this question without remaining somewhat on the periphery and saying all the various things that can affect the salivary conditional reflex. In general, I find that the salivary conditional reflex, like other conditional reflexes, is subject to things that happen in the dog's environment. I mean, if he is in a fight, or if something disturbs him the night before, that will tend to have an effect on the differentiation in his salivary conditioning. With a number of dogs in which we keep the conditions constant, we have gotten, from day to day, very constant salivary conditional reflexes. I think it depends also on the number of different kinds of stimuli that you use, and whether you are introducing stressful situations in the animal that disturb him, but I can only say that usually, without seeing evident disturbances in the dog's life, we have been able to get nearly constant salivary conditional reflexes.

Question: What is the relationship between the difficulty in extinguishing the cardiac rate to the Selye adaptation syndrome stress concept, and to what extent do you think Selye's stress is a result of conditioning?

Gantt: I think you certainly can condition stress. Stress is brought about, first, by some kind of inborn reactivity; e.g., fright, pain, or a variety of things, many of which happen very early in life. Whatever is connected with this will then reproduce this stress. In the case of the human being, the function of generalization is much greater than it is in any other animal.

The second signaling system, which was the name Pavlov gave

to the language function, provides a mechanism for very widespread generalization. To give a kind of schematic answer to this, the original stress will produce all the visceral reactions, hormonal secretions, etc. As we showed in some of the laboratory dogs, the room, the people, the food, the tones, and a number of related things, become connected with the stress. Now we can easily conjecture that in the human being, not only these objects, but also the *names* for them become connected.

We therefore have the mechanism in the human being for a large variety of things which depend upon the particular individual; what things, or how many, we cannot say. Many situations can produce the same reaction as the original stress situation. As has been shown, it may be very difficult to extinguish these, and certainly the individual himself may be entirely unconscious of what is producing the changes in his visceral system.

Question: I was very much interested in the comment that people can be more powerful stimuli than other stimuli we are accustomed to use, and I was wondering how much connection this might have with the observation that many people with mental illness, such as schizophrenics, are withdrawn in the company of other people. Could this mean that other people are too strong stimuli for them? You say that this is important for therapy. Could you elaborate a little on some of the connections here that you see?

Gantt: A person can take on the effect of almost any agent with which he is connected. He can take on the effect of a drug with which he is connected—of any situation with which he is connected. What we have shown in the laboratory, which seems to me the basic thing, is that the mere presence of the person can be a most powerful stimulus. We demonstrated this experimentally, for example, in the catatonic dog, V3. V3 was raised in the laboratory, lived to be fourteen, and died in the laboratory just last year. Some of Dr. Newton's experiments with this dog showed that a person merely sitting in the room with him would bring his heart rate down from around 160 to 40. If the person petted him, his heart rate would go still lower, to around about 30. His blood pressure would also drop. These relationships are special to the particular person or to the particular dog. They show that the individual has this ability—the influencing of one person by another. This is as powerful a stimulus as a real cardiac drug may be. In fact, the presence of a person may, in a neurotic dog, lower the heart and blood pressure more profoundly than even a specific such as acetylcholine.

THE CHALLENGE OF PAVLOVIAN CONDITIONING AND EXPERIMENTAL NEUROSES IN ANIMALS*

Howard S. Liddell, Ph.D.

In *Moses and Monotheism* Freud says, "Neurosis seems to be a human privilege." We challenge this statement. Perhaps if Freud were a young man today, and in possession of the facts about to be detailed concerning experimental neurosis, he would challenge his own statement! He once expressed interest in the possibilities of primate research in disclosing the biological origins of the period of latency.

The challenge of Pavlovian conditioning and experimental neuroses in animals has its basis in the natural history of emotion. Stanley Cobb (1958) says: "Many psychologists and psychiatrists who deal with human beings become engulfed in the complexity of their material and never become acquainted with the simple and important facts of 'natural history.'[1] Training in the simple biology of barnyard and forest is a great educational advantage. The fact that many leading psychiatrists are urban products, knowing little of these biological fundamentals, has led to much misunderstanding of what an instinct really is, and also to much vague use of such terms as 'instinctual.' "

---

* The editors gratefully acknowledge the generous assistance of Dr. Ulric Moore in revising this paper after the death of Dr. Liddell in 1962.

[1] In similar vein, Leon J. Saul (1962) has said, "I do know that much that we struggle to solve by free associations *alone* becomes intelligible if we shift our focus from the human psyche, expressed in the office through speech, to the overt behavior of our animal cousins. Though inferior to us intellectually, we can learn much from them about the emotions, including the nature of maturing and maturity, for animals react without disguise."

Figure 1. Our laboratory for Pavlovian conditioning of sheep and goats in the early nineteen thirties.

And so, back to the barnyard, where for the past forty years we have investigated Pavlovian conditioning and experimental neuroses in the sheep and goat, although we did not neglect the pig and the dog. The obdurate and highly intelligent pig pitted his wits against ours, and even though we succeeded in establishing classical salivary and motor conditioned reflexes (and experimental neuroses) we, like Pavlov, abandoned this gifted animal. Pavlov (1934), recounting his experiences with the pig in his attempts to secure gastric juice from a fistula for therapeutic purposes, said: "It screamed at the top of its voice and all work in the laboratory was impossible. All attempts to soothe it were in vain and we gave it to the attendants for an Easter present."

If, as we believe, Pavlovian conditioning is primarily concerned with the emotional context of behavior, rather than with learning or intelligence in the pedagogical sense, we may define a positive conditioned reflex as follows: It is an emotionally charged episode of behavior bracketed between two primitive, stereotyped, forced reactions. These forced reactions are unconditioned reflexes in Pavlov's sense. The first is the investigatory reflex or "what-is-it" reflex. Henry Head called it vigilance. The second is the forced reaction that is elicited to food or an irritating substance (such as 0.1% HCl) in the mouth, or to mild electric shock to the forelimb.

The onset of the conditioned stimulus elicits a spike of alertness

Figure 2. Reaction to mild electric shock on the foreleg of a well-conditioned sheep. This is the unconditioned reflex used in establishing positive and negative conditioned reflexes in sheep and goat.

or vigilance, followed by steadily increasing impatience, until terminated by the forced reaction to reinforcement (food or irritant in the mouth, or electric shock to a limb). *All negative conditioned reflexes are based upon previously established positive conditioned reflexes by omitting the reinforcement at the end of the signal.* By thus omitting the terminal forced reaction the nervous tension is steadily increased from signal to signal. The animal maintains its self-imposed restraint at rapidly increasing physiological cost. Often, in our experience, during the extinction of a positive conditioned reflex by regular repetition of the signal every minute without the expected reinforcement, loss of emotional control suddenly supervenes and we observe the agitated type of experimental neurosis that persists for life.[2]

I now propose to take you on an illustrated excursion into the past, reviewing our findings in conditioning hundreds of sheep and goats over a period of forty years.

Our laboratory for conditioning as it appeared in the early thirties is shown in Figure 1. It closely follows Pavlov's original plan. The animal

---

[2] Special "deconditioning" procedures can, however, terminate such neuroses (Masserman, 1943; Napalkov & Karas, 1957; Wolpe, 1958). [Editors' note]

Sheep #7

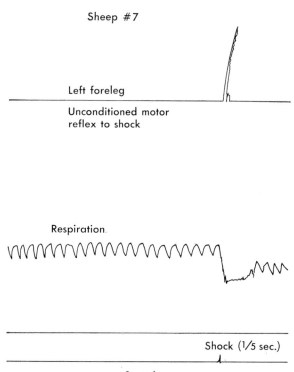

Left foreleg

Unconditioned motor
reflex to shock

Respiration.

Shock (1/5 sec.)

Seconds

Figure 3. A kymograph tracing of the foreleg flexion to a brief
electric shock shown in Figure 2. Note the brief, precise flexion
movement indicated by the upstroke of the myograph lever and
the brief interruption of the regular movements of respiration.

(dog, sheep, or goat) has learned to stand quietly on a table. Loops
suspended from an overhead beam pass under the limbs. This arrange-
ment was devised for the experimenter's convenience in Pavlov's early
investigation of the secretion of gastric juice, where a flask could be
placed under the fistula in the animal's belly wall. The dog, always eager
to please his master, soon learns to jump on the table and remain quietly
in the "Pavlov frame," sometimes for hours. With the sheep and goat,
however, a different situation obtains. A period of violent but fruitless
struggling to escape is soon followed by the tense quiet of conditioned
restraint. In the case of the adult male ram or billy goat one year of age,
unremitting resistance to the restraining harness continues. The ram, for
instance, will bellow, paw rapidly with the forefoot, and butt in response
to signal and shock, and will "take a swipe" at the experimenter if he
approaches during the conditioning experiment. At three months of age,

by contrast, the young male is as docile as the female in the conditioning situation.

Returning to Figure 1, we can see that a bracelet is attached to the sheep's foreleg through which the mild, reinforcing electric shock is administered, and from the forefoot a string running under the table actuates a myograph lever inscribing the movements of the limb on a kymograph in the adjoining room. Similarly, movements of the head and of respiration are recorded.

Let us now experimentally dissect a positive motor conditioned reflex in the sheep with the laboratory arrangements just described. A brief electric shock of six volts is applied to the animal's foreleg. It is so weak that it can scarcely be felt as a faint tingling when applied to the moistened fingers, and feels only mildly disagreeable on the tip of the tongue. But to the sheep or goat it is a disturbing stimulus. In the early days of training, the sheep leaps upward at the shock and struggles violently with movement of all four limbs. With repeated experiences, however, these ineffectual movements of running away are reduced to a single, brisk flexion of the stimulated limb, as shown in Figure 2. If the flexion of the foreleg and the movements of respiration are recorded, it will be observed (See Figure 3) that the previously developed self-imposed restraint is now so concentrated and precise that the breathing movements resume their former amplitude and rhythm within a few seconds.

Continuing our dissection of the conditioned reflex, we discover that the sheep's reaction to any signal (such as a tactile stimulus) that constantly precedes the shock to his foreleg undergoes a process of concentration and refinement. This process involves the same change from diffused to focused motor reaction that we observed when a shock was actually administered to the foreleg. When the conditioned reflex first develops, the animal, in response to the signal, exhibits the same ineffectual movements of running away. But with practice this too becomes precise and localized, as illustrated in Figure 4. Here, a middle-aged sheep with many years of conditioning experience has acquired a tactile conditioned reflex reinforced by the usual shock to the foreleg. A tambour provided with blunt metal points is attached to a shaved area on the rump. By rhythmically pressing a bulb the experimenter inflates the tambour and thus exerts light pressure, once a second, upon the shaved skin. This rhythmical pressure, applied for a few seconds, is followed by a single shock to the foreleg. We see that precise flexions of the foreleg follow the mild rhythmical tactile stimuli to the skin on the sheep's back.

The animal subjected to this kind of Pavlovian conditioning is under experimentally controlled stress. Its conditioned behavior derives from the innate "fight-flight" pattern of Cannon's emergency reaction. *Its inevitable*

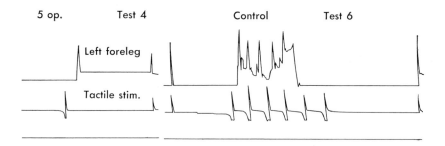

Figure 4. Kymograph tracing of a well-established tactile conditioned reflex in the sheep. Rythmical tactile stimulation of a small shaved area on the animal's rump for a few seconds has always been followed by a shock on the foreleg. Note the precise flexions of the foreleg in response to the light taps on the skin of the sheep's back.

consequence, if long enough continued even at its mildest intensity, is experimental neurosis.

The *objective* manifestations of experimental neuroses are basically the same for dog, pig, goat, and man. The behavior of the neurotically ill individual, whether animal or man, is ineffectual and unrealistic. It limits him in meeting his total life situation *in its historical continuity.* Patterns of frustrating behavior persist, of their own momentum, year after year in sheep and goat, and in man, for decade after decade.

Figure 5, in the left-hand column, shows the reaction of a normal sheep to the buzzer. The buzzer starts, and the animal lowers his head and quickly flexes his foreleg.

The right-hand column of Figure 5, however, shows what happens when the neurotic sheep hears the buzzer. Now notice the exaggerated startle response to the sound of the buzzer, and the rising and over-reactive diffused motor reaction. Figure 6 shows this graphically. Notice how soon after the buzzer and shock the normal animal quiets down. But the neurotic animal shows diffused agitation, overreaction of the disturbed forelimb, and irregular breathing.

Figure 7 is interesting. Here is a sheep reacting to bell, no shock; buzzer, shock. There is differentiation here. He reacts a little with the left foreleg to the bell, but not much; but then to the buzzer before shock, a precise reaction. Notice the minimum number of head movements; notice the regular respiration as we slow down the kymograph. Notice the steadiness of the heart: 66, 66, 60, 66 beats per minute.

In Figure 8, we have this same animal, six months later. Here we see

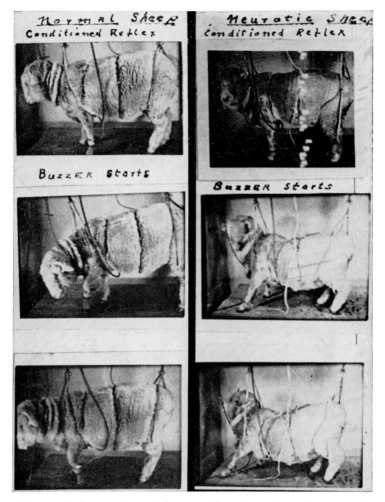

Figure 5. Comparison of the conditioned reactions of a normal and an experimentally neurotic sheep to the sound of a buzzer signaling an approaching shock to the foreleg. The three pictures arranged vertically on the left show the reaction of the normal sheep to the buzzer. The pictures on the right from top to bottom show the violent struggling of the neurotic sheep to the same buzzer signal.

the diffused, agitated pattern of the classical experimental neurosis, continual head movement, bleating, left foreleg overreacting to the metronome. He had been taught to give no reaction to the metronome at 50 beats per minute, but here it shows that he cannot inhibit, and all differentiation between signals for shock and for no shock has been

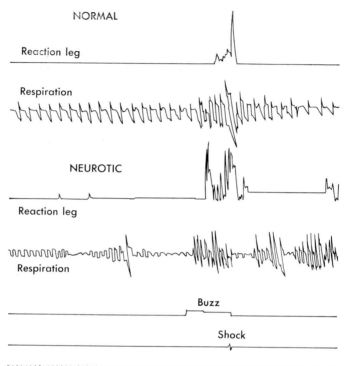

NORMAL

Reaction leg

Respiration

NEUROTIC

Reaction leg

Respiration

Buzz

Shock

Seconds

Figure 6. Comparison of the conditioned and unconditioned motor reactions of a normal and a neurotic sheep to the same signal (or conditioned stimulus). The respirations are recorded from breathing through a mask, eliminating extraneous muscular movements. Note the exaggerated reactions of the foreleg and the highly irregular respiration of the neurotic sheep.

eliminated. The heart beat (96, 96, 100, 90) is irregular, with many premature beats. Moreover, the heart of this animal is disturbed in the barn at night. The animal also loses its normal gregariousness and when alarmed by marauding dogs will not run off with the flock, but in another direction, and the neurotic sheep will often be mauled by the dogs.

Our first neurotic sheep, a castrated male, lived to the age of thirteen and a half years. We found in early studies of these experimental neuroses that they did not curtail the animal's normal life span.

The animal shown in Figure 9, having been put in the frame, could not forbear from keeping his left foreleg in nervous agitation, and when he was "an old man"—when he was just premortem—we had to lift him

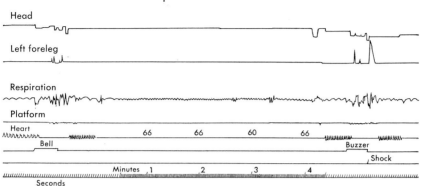

Sheep #52

Figure 7. Showing the normal conditioned deportment of Sheep 52. This animal had been thoroughly conditioned to a 10-second signal every 5 minutes. The positive signal was a buzzer followed by shock; the negative signal, a bell never followed by shock. The positive and negative signals alternated every 5 minutes. Thus the sheep was conditioned to the waiting period of 5 minutes between signals and, at the same time, to the specific buzzer signal for shock and to the bell signal for no shock. In this tracing the bell for 10 seconds without shock is followed after 5 minutes by the buzzer for 10 seconds terminated by the usual shock.

From top to bottom the traces record the movements of the head, conditioned left foreleg, respiration and the animal's movements on the platform (pneumatically recorded). Then come heart rate, signal, shock, and time in seconds and minutes. Although in this particular test there is a small conditioned reaction both to bell and to buzzer, the vigorous flexion to shock after buzzer clearly appears on the second line from the top.

This normal animal's self-imposed restraint is clearly shown by absence of head and forelimb movements during the 5-minute waiting period between signals. Note the slow, steady heart rates of 66, 66, 60, and 66 beats per minute during the 4 succeeding minutes of the waiting period.

onto the table and adjust the straps; but his leg would still keep up its fidgeting (See Figure 10).

The typical goat's free foreleg flexion at the signal can be seen in Figure 11.

Using the following signal: metronome once a second for ten seconds, then shock; two-minute interval and again ten-second signal, then shock, two-minute interval, and so on, twenty signals a day, five days a week, month after month after month, finally results in the other type of experi-

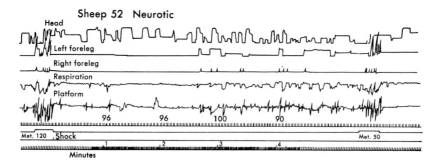

Figure 8. Showing the neurotic manifestations of the same sheep as in Figure 7. This tracing is from a portion of the usual one-hour conditioning test. She is now chronically neurotic and will remain so until her death at 10 years of age. Her experimental neurosis manifests itself as diffuse agitation affecting her behavior in laboratory, barn, and pasture. *This neurotic agitation is not limited to the laboratory situation.* See text for details.

The nine lines of this tracing beginning at the top record movements of the head, left "conditioned" foreleg, right foreleg, respiration, and movements on the pneumatically recording platform. Then, as in Figure 7, come heart beats per minute, signal, shock, and time in seconds and minutes. Note the absence of restraint as evidenced by vigorous, repeated head movements, vehement and repeated movements of the conditioned left foreleg both to positive and negative signals and smaller fidgeting movements during the 5-minute waiting period. After long training the animal cannot distinguish between a new pair of signals, namely, the metronome at 120 beats per minute followed by shock and the metronome at 50 beats per minute without shock. Not only the conditioned left foreleg, but the right foreleg also is flexed during both signal and waiting period. At shock all four limbs are in movement as if the animal were "running in place." General motor restlessness is shown by the continual movements of the platform. The respiratory record (fourth line from the top) is obscured by the animal's struggling to escape. Now that experimental neurosis has been precipitated, in her case quite suddenly, Sheep 52 exhibits a rapid and irregular pulse. During the five-minute interval between signals the heart rates are 96, 96, 100, and 90 beats per minute in successive minutes.

mental neurosis in which there is overreaction of the parasympathetic division of the nervous system. The animal is thus quite rigid, turning his head as if it were on stiff springs (see Figure 12).

When experimental neurosis is induced by difficult differentiation, it results in overactivity of the sympathetic division of the nervous system.

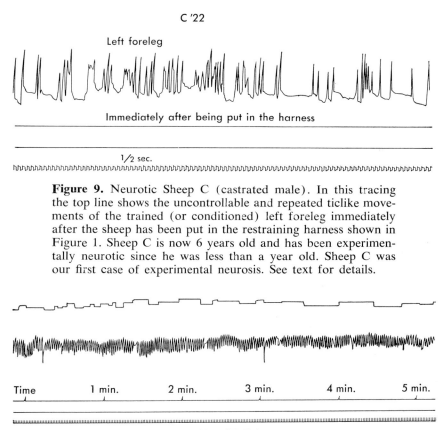

C '22

Left foreleg

Immediately after being put in the harness

1/2 sec.

Figure 9. Neurotic Sheep C (castrated male). In this tracing the top line shows the uncontrollable and repeated ticlike movements of the trained (or conditioned) left foreleg immediately after the sheep has been put in the restraining harness shown in Figure 1. Sheep C is now 6 years old and has been experimentally neurotic since he was less than a year old. Sheep C was our first case of experimental neurosis. See text for details.

Time   1 min.   2 min.   3 min.   4 min.   5 min.

C '22 5-Ⅲ-'34

Figure 10. Neurotic Sheep C when over 13 years old at time of experiment. He died a few days after this experiment. He was so feeble that he had to be lifted onto the table and the loops under the limbs prevented him from sinking to the floor. He showed obvious signs of senility but the feeble ticlike movements of the trained foreleg continued for 5 minutes without the usual conditioned stimuli. Note the occasional deep respirations and pauses in the second line from the top. These irregularities of respiration are observed in both animal and human neuroses.

This is summarized in Figure 13. Figure 14 shows the famous Brown Billy flexing his leg at the sound of the metronome clicking once a second and recorded by suitable instrumentation.

We believed at first that we had obtained a clear differentiation—one syndrome for the overactive sympathetic type of experimental neurosis, and another syndrome for the overactive parasympathetic type of experi-

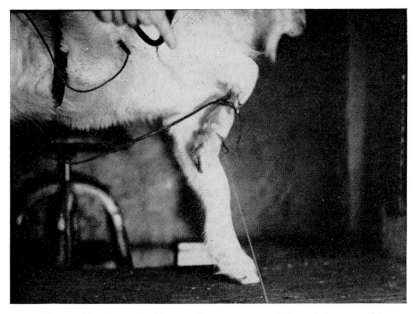

Figure 11. Goat 2. This animal was conditioned to a rigid time schedule. The metronome at 60 beats per minute (M60) was sounded for 10 seconds followed by the usual mild shock to the foreleg. Every 2 minutes, for 10 cycles, the metronome was sounded for 10 seconds, followed by shock. The precise flexion of the foreleg to the clicking of the metronome is shown here.

mental neurosis. But we had to give up the idea of two quite diverse syndromes because of results from our work starting with the younger animals. The subjects of this work were sheep and goats with twins of the same sex. Figure 15 shows the mother sheep with one twin. The twins are tested in separate rooms at the same time, one in a room by itself and the other in a room with its mother. Soon this second twin is quite at ease. He dutifully flexes his leg while looking at his mother standing by. If she is lying down, he may jump on her at the shock, for he is free to do as he pleases.

It is the same with the goat mother and kid (Figure 16). So long as the kid can be near her, he will oblige us by picking up this leg-lifting trick, but it is no more than a trick to him. Emotionally he is not upset by the conditioning.

In Figure 17 we have the other little twin kid by himself in a room of the same size. Here the little animal forms, as it were, a Pavlov frame for

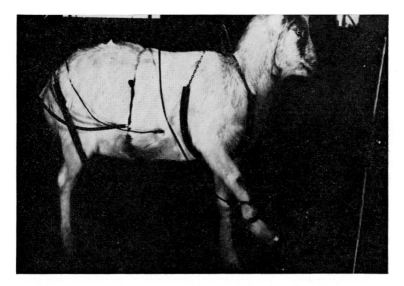

Figure 12. Goat 2. The rigid extension of the foreleg at the clicking of the metronome preceding the shock developed after 1000 metronome signals spaced 2 minutes apart. This awkward extension of the trained foreleg replacing the former precise, graceful flexion shown in Figure 11 resembles the neurotic disability of writer's or telegrapher's cramp. See details in text. This neurosis persisted until the animal's death 5 years later following brain surgery (to test James Papez's hypothesis of the visceral brain).

himself. He gives up the free exploration of the room. Separated from his mother, he stands quietly and flexes the leg. But if we continue with this little kid (Figure 18)—every two minutes we dim the lights in the room for ten seconds, then administer the shock—the eventual outcome is as if he were in the restraining Pavlov harness. He has made his own harness conditioned self-restraint, and the typical parasympathetic type of experimental neurosis has developed.

Another observation we made was that the presence of the experimenter also influences the lone animal's behavior. In the case of an animal we had observed through a one-way screen, we found that if an observer was placed in the corner of the room, the animal gave up exploring the room and became very quiet. (Vocalization is very significant in experimental neurosis. In the agitated type of neurosis the sheep bleats all the time, and in the other type it becomes very quiet.) The little animal edged toward the experimenter a few steps at a time, backed

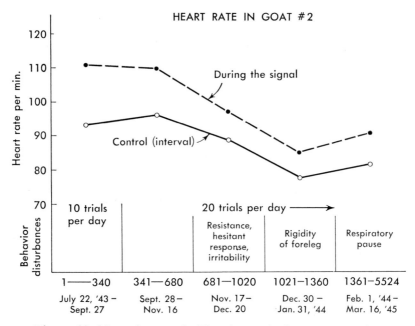

Figure 13. Neurotic goat 2. The change in heart rate at the metronome signals and during the 2-minute intervals between signals is shown in the upper two lines of the graph. The onset of the disturbances in behavior with the gradual onset of experimental neurosis is shown in the blocks from left to right at the bottom of the figure. See text.

away, got closer and closer, backed away—a typical exhibition of ambivalence. In one experiment, after twenty signals the animal jumped onto the lap of the observer.

We were also able to compare total locomotion during a fifty-minute period, of twin lambs, three weeks old, on exposure to the regimen of signal (dimmed light for ten seconds) and shock. At first each of them wandered all over, but the little lamb isolated was less lively than the animal with its mother. Later, we observed the little lamb by itself making his own "Pavlov frame." He crept along the wall and was very quiet throughout the session. Still later, he moved just back and forth along one wall. Finally, the animal had imposed self-restraint upon himself to the effect that he was completely motionless during the experimental hour. While the other lamb still maintained his liberty, this one had been emotionally "traumatized." This amounted to a sentence of death on him, for, as we found to our dismay, those animals who are run by themselves die within the year, usually within a few months, whereas the twins who

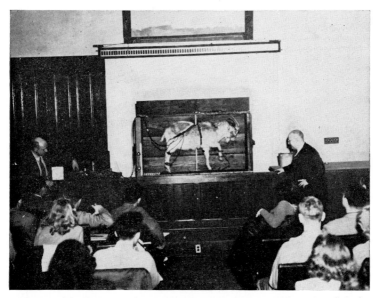

Figure 14. Lecture demonstration of the conditioned reflexes of neurotic goat Brown Billy. He died in the winter of 1962 at 15 years of age and had been experimentally neurotic since his first year. We demonstrated his neurotic performance before many groups of neuropsychiatrists.

are run with the mother do not. Those who run alone die from various causes—dehydration, excessive parasites, and so on.

The foregoing illustrates a completely new aspect of conditioning: mutual Pavlovian conditioning. Remember that conventional Pavlovian conditioning is forced upon the animal. He plays a passive role. He is forced to remain in place; external restraint leads to self-imposed restraint. He has to receive alarm signals at our convenience, not at his, and his reaction is stereotyped.

But when we start exploring the mutual relations between the newborn kid or lamb and its mother, we call this *mutual conditioning,* which involves what has come to be known as operant or "Skinner-box" conditioning, where the animal can press a lever to make the environment obey his action.

My colleagues, Dr. and Mrs. Ulric Moore, have done obstetrical service around the clock, night after night, when the new kids and lambs were being born, and have studied them with moving pictures and with careful personal notes as to just what transpires in the relation between the newborn and its mother sheep or goat. Mrs. Moore writes,

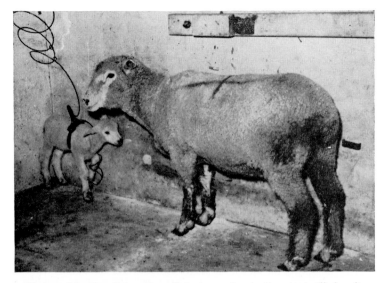

Figure 15. Conditioned reflex in a lamb "protected" by its mother's presence. The lights in the room are dimmed for 10 seconds followed by mild shock to the foreleg. As explained in the text, the mutual conditioning of mother and young, following birth, protects the little animal from the traumatic effects of Pavlovian conditioning when the mother is present during the experiment.

Mutual conditioning in the sheep and goat is accomplished through all the senses, smell, taste, body contact, hearing, seeing, and by the place sense as well; that is, animals become used to where to find their young and the young to where the mother is, and any disarranging of a population of a group of mothers and their young is very disturbing to both mother and young. When mutual conditioning is accomplished in the normal manner, no inhibiting is required of the young by the mother during the first days of life. When inhibiting is eventually required by the mother (not allowing the young to nurse), the process is very gradual (which is just the opposite of Pavlovian conditioning, which is all dumped on the animal at our convenience).

Any inhibition imposed by the mother is done in such a way that the young expects satisfaction in the near future. Any refusal of nursing is indicated by clear-cut signals such as a motion of the leg that covers the udder. There is never any confusion as to what is intended. Body contacts with the mother are never refused. She at all times permits the young to make contact with her in any way that it may desire. It may sleep close to her, or in play jump on her, or

Figure 16. Conditioned reflex in a kid "protected" by its mother's presence. The experimental conditions are the same as in Figure 15. In both cases the little animal, in its mother's presence, is subjected to 20 "darkness" signals of 10 seconds duration, separated by 2-minute waiting periods with the room fully lighted.

after nursing may stand under her head or body. Termination of the mutual conditioning is very gradual and is effected by a widening circle as the young becomes less dependent upon the nursing process for its food.

Now the key to this mutual conditioning seems to be an interplay of pleasurable behavior patterns [you never find the word "pleasure" in Pavlovian conditioning] so that mutual pleasurable stimulation is involved throughout. The signals for the food to be offered are consistent and always followed by what they imply. This results in digestive readiness and completely relaxed resting periods since no ambivalence has been aroused.

Thus the mother conditions the newborn lamb or kid in this mutual interchange of responses that prevents the development of experimental neurosis.

I want to mention some other work we have been doing. Figure 19 shows evidence that specific metabolic effects appear in the horn growth as a result of experimental neurosis. Sherrington severed a cutaneous nerve and used fingernail parings to show that fingernail growth was affected during nerve sectioning and regeneration. In our regimen, horn

Figure 17. Kid separated from its mother is subjected to the same conditioning routine as the lamb and kid in Figures 15 and 16. Without the presence of the mother it will succumb to the type of experimental neurosis exhibited by Goat 2, as shown in Figures 12 and 13.

Figure 18. Kid separated from its mother during conditioning according to the rigid time schedule of 20 "darkness" signals of 10 seconds separated by 2-minute intervals. The neurosis duplicates in detail the manifestations shown in neurotic Goat 2.

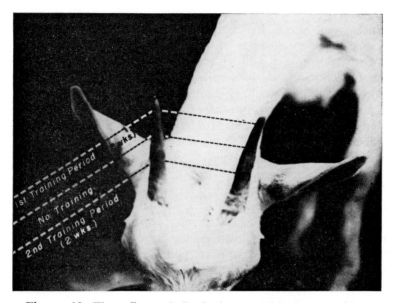

Figure 19. The effect of Pavlovian conditioning on horn growth, showing arrest of horn growth during periods of conditioning.

growth is inhibited during the first training period. The horn bulges and becomes glossy during the nontraining period, and then is inhibited again when training is resumed. We are making some fascinating studies on the effect of these disabling emotional experiences on horn growth and on general development as well.

For example, we are now engaged in a foster care program in which a mother goat with her own kid will be forced to adopt a lamb of the same age. The mother will allow this lamb to nurse because she is in a stanchion and cannot butt it away. The foster lamb will try his best to play with the mother's own kid and be a kid among kids but he tires out too soon; he doesn't develop as rapidly. In other instances we have also had kids adopted by sheep mothers, sometimes along with their own lambs as siblings. We have a kid, Chris (he is now a billy goat a year old) who was adopted by a sheep. He has never considered himself anything other than a sheep. He plays with the sheep, he runs around with the sheep, he has no contact with the goats. Now his horns have been so imperfectly developed that all we ever find are two little bloody knobs on his head. As soon as they start to grow, the horns are knocked off in play.

We have also been doing some work that involves the production of experimental immobilization, or "animal hypnosis," of the sheep and goat. You throw the animal on its side, you squeeze the neck in a firm grip.

Feeling the head coming back, you gradually release the grip, and the animal is immobilized. Its righting reflexes are physiologically blocked by this deep pressure, and most of the conditioned reflexes are blocked too. We would press a bulb which supplied a skin spot. This would be followed by a shock to the foreleg. The conditioned reflex which was previously established would be diminished. The point is that this cataleptic-like state in these experimentally immobilized animals is a very sensitive indicator of their emotional balance, because bottle-fed, mother-isolated lambs or kids, or kids and lambs that are adopted by a female of their own species or of cross species, cannot be immobilized. This is an excellent exploratory lead.

The only application to human hypnosis that may work out in the future is what we accidentally discovered back in 1943. When an animal negatively conditioned (no shock to metronome 120 beats to the minute) is immobilized by being thrown on the floor with pressure still on the neck, the metronome will take over from the hand pressure and you can keep the animal under for fifteen minutes. Even with a class of two hundred students who have been told to scream, yell, and stamp their feet, the sheep will stay immobilized.

In recent years, as John Lilly has pointed out, we have opened a new door in our research in human behavior:

> In working with electrodes implanted in specific areas in a monkey's brain, one can observe reactions which resemble extremely closely the various things seen in and felt by humans under extreme conditions. Animal tests now show these to be true emotions felt by the animal. Work with humans stimulating these same systems has corroborated conclusions from animal research. These reactions are indeed true emotions rather than sham or pseudo-affective reactions.

This leads us to the crux of the matter from my point of view: our challenge to the psychoanalysts and to ourselves. Consider the situation in Pavlov's and Freud's day. They were medical contemporaries. They were raised in the old mechanistic physiology. Both of them could not get inside the human calvarium or the animal calvarium. The brain in those early days operated in secret within its skull. Now this has all changed. Whereas Pavlov was forced into a speculative neurology based on Sherrington's neurologic doctrine of integrative action of the nervous system, Freud, who was a skilled neurophysiologist in his day, rejected this approach and invented psychodynamics. Today, both Pavlov's speculative neurology and Freud's purely speculative psychodynamics are passé: they are old-fashioned. Times have changed. We are in an era of objectivity. A real neurology is replacing the speculative.

REFERENCES

COBB, S. *Foundations of neuropsychiatry.* Baltimore: Williams & Wilkins, 1958.

MASSERMAN, J. H. *Behavior and neurosis.* Chicago: U. of Chicago Press, 1943.

NAPALKOV, A. V., & KARAS, A. YA. Elimination of pathological conditioned reflex connections in the experimental hypertensive state. *Zh. vyssh. nervn. Deiatel'.,* 1957, *7,* 402–409.

PAVLOV, I. P., 1934. Quoted in Liddell, H. S. Conditioned reflex method and experimental neurosis. In J. McV. Hunt (Ed.), *Personality and the behavior disorders* (Vol. I). New York: Ronald, 1944.

SAUL, L. J. Psychosocial medicine and observations of animals. *Psychosom. Med.,* 1962, *24,* 58–68.

WOLPE, J. *Psychotherapy by reciprocal inhibition.* Stanford: Stanford University Press, 1958.

DISCUSSION

Question: I should like to ask three questions. How does repetition produce a neurosis? Also, would you amplify your concepts of what constitutes a sympathetic and a parasympathetic neurosis? I am not quite sure that I understand the difference. And a third question is related to the effects of mothering on the infant. How does this work? Of course, this is a tremendously important field. It has been worked on by Spitz, among others, and I am curious about what information Dr. Liddell can give us on why mothering should have its particular effects.

Liddell: In answer to the first of these questions, we were much puzzled and surprised indeed to get the experimental neurosis by the reiteration of positive signals, with no element of conflict, since psychopathologists have stressed conflict so much. Here you have only reiteration of signal, reinforced in a fixed time pattern, and it seems that this is a more basic cause of neurosis than conflict. I wonder if it may not be related to the repetitive core of the neuromechanism observed in play, and if our neuroses may not be a distorted or deviant development of the primitive play pattern. Now, we are still puzzled about the two forms of experimental neurosis in adult sheep and goat, that is, those conditioned from three months on, as to why, when the signals are spaced at various intervals apart, you would get sympathetic overactivity chronically, and, on the other hand, with regular two-minute signals, you get this preponderance of parasympathetic chronic distortion. We do not know. And it is an exceedingly interesting matter to investigate. It is interesting that Dr. Spitz was mentioned, because it was on the impetus of his work that we began this program. His pictures of the hospitalized children are dismal to see. He's discussed this at great length with us, and we owe our inspiration to Dr. Spitz specifically.

Now about the maternal neonate relationship. This is an exceedingly complicated matter, because we have taken the animal away from its mother and made it quite content with human companionship. In fact, in the early days, one of our female lambs was adopted by the family of a graduate associate who had a little daughter of five, and a German shepherd and a cocker spaniel. This lamb was the child's companion. It once got its throat torn competing with the German shepherd over a pork chop, which it could not have eaten anyway. The lamb would wander in fresh grass up to its knees and never graze. It liked bread crust, dog biscuit, and discards from restaurants.

We once found ourselves with four orphan goats, raised in a little "orphanage" and fed with a milk bottle and nipples, and milk pan and nipples. When we tried to get this small group of four orphans to join the larger flock of twenty-five, the four of them selected their female as the leader. She went and surveyed the female chosen by the larger flock, and they locked horns. When she led her little flock aside, and we chased the large flock out, they would not follow the large flock. When the three of us, Dr. Eleanor Gibson, Dr. Moore, and myself, went out to take notes and spread over the field, we each found these goats grazing around our feet. Konrad Lorenz once said that a female goose had permitted him to help her build her nest, and he considered himself an honorary goose. And so we have become honorary sheep and honorary goats.

Question: I would like to ask Dr. Liddell for a clarification of his remark about the failure of the neurosis to diminish or extinguish over many years. I was unclear whether he was referring to neuroses that were unreinforced during these intervening years or were reinforced. If so —that is, if they really did not extinguish over these years, is this not, perhaps, a species difference, possibly restricted to the animal he studied, since there is evidence in some reports that neuroses in animals will extinguish if they are studied sufficiently long?

Liddell: Natural remission of experimental neurosis is brief and unpredictable, and we cannot pin it down as clinicians would like to. We do know that a complete rest, not only from the laboratory but also from the familiar farm environments, is of no benefit. We gave several of our neurotic sheep a three-year holiday, we moved our laboratory two or three miles, or a mile away, we had a new laboratory building, a new grazing pasture, but once these animals returned to the laboratory, within a week or two the remission was over. They were back to the standard neurotic pattern.

INDIVIDUAL DIFFERENCES IN CONDITIONING AND ASSOCIATED TECHNIQUES

Cyril M. Franks, Ph.D.

We know a fair amount, on an empirical basis, about individual differences in the ability to form, maintain, and extinguish conditioned responses; much data are also available concerning individual differences in performance on a wide variety of other laboratory tests. Much of these data are consistent with, and predictable from, a comparatively small number of theories, most of which stem back, at least in part, to certain Pavlovian concepts, especially those pertaining to inhibition. The term "inhibition" is perhaps an unfortunate one since it is widely used by psychologists and psychiatrists of many diverse schools of thought and also by physiologists. The typical psychiatric usage to denote the behavior of the introverted and withdrawn individual has little or nothing in common with the more precise usage of the neurophysiologist, and the neurophysiological usage has only occasional (but increasing) communality with the at-the-present largely hypothetical and molar usage of Pavlovian and other learning theorists. In some circumstances (such as the terminology of Eysenck and his associates), central inhibition in the so-called Pavlovian sense is conceptually associated with the absence of behavioral inhibition in the psychiatric sense. The matter is further complicated by the infusion of a variety of qualifying adjectives such as *retroactive, differential, basal, reciprocal, internal, external, reactive,* and *conditioned.*

It must be firmly recognized that Pavlov's concern was not just with conditioning as such but with central processes and the principles governing all aspects of their functioning and their behavioral manifestations. Of necessity, Pavlov had to *infer* the existence and properties of these processes from the study and observation of peripheral activities such as salivation, and had to rely almost exclusively upon the techniques of classical conditioning to achieve his goal. Nowadays we are in the fortunate position of having techniques available for the more direct study of these central processes, techniques which, hopefully, will contribute to the eventual understanding of such processes directly in terms of brain physiology, histochemistry, and other fundamental biological sciences.

Such speculation, and more certainly such a research program, is hardly within the province or capacity of the psychologist. The more immediate tasks for the psychologist would appear to include (1) the establishment of the generality of these various concepts of inhibition and the amount of variance taken up by inhibition-based principles in any specific task; (2) the extension of classical conditioning techniques to more meaningful and organismically consequential units than eye blinks, knee jerks, galvanic skin reflexes, and the like (the present upsurge of Soviet emphasis on semantic conditioning and unconscious visceral activity, so admirably documented by Razran [1961], indicates the desirable new look in this respect); (3) the extension of Pavlovian and modern learning theory principles to an increasingly wide range of psychophysiological phenomena and behavioral situations inside the laboratory and outside; and (4) the study of individual differences in response to the various forms of behavior therapy and their relation to individual differences in laboratory test performance in such a way that it will be possible to predict with some accuracy an individual's likelihood of success in any particular form of behavior theory.

INDIVIDUAL DIFFERENCES IN CONDITIONING

If we confine our remarks to man, and thus avoid the necessity for any assumptions of phylogenetic continuity, it appears reasonably certain that anxious individuals are able to form a variety of conditioned responses more quickly and more strongly than normal people or than patients who are less anxious. Once formed, these responses are more persistent and less amenable to extinction procedures. There is much less certainty or agreement as to why this should be so. Spence and his associates believe that this state of affairs arises because of anxiety as a drive, Eysenck and his associates maintain that the habit strength or inhibition component of Hull's equation is more usually responsible. But, whatever the rationale, the fact apparently remains (Franks, C. M., 1960).

There is some evidence to suggest that, under certain circumstances, normal introverted individuals are better conditioners and are slower to extinguish than extraverted, and that introverted neurotics are better conditioners than extraverted. The evidence is far from conclusive; furthermore, the generality of these results to reflexes other than the eye blink, and possibly the galvanic skin reflex, remains to be established (Eysenck, 1960a). Even when these two responses are considered, it is not adequately known how much the relationship is masked by other variables such as motivation, the subject's attitude, the instructions given, the modality of the conditioned stimulus, and the intensities and relationships of the various stimuli concerned. Nevertheless, it is apparent that there are wide individual differences in conditioning and that these differences are at least partially related to other personality factors.

There are two basic and related areas in which problems most urgently require solution: first, that of the existence of a general factor of conditioning, or perhaps a small number of group factors, possibly one pertaining more to the central nervous system and one pertaining more to the autonomic nervous system; second, *whether* it is legitimate to refer to a person's conditionability—a concept for which there may be no practical utility if, in any specific situation, much of the variance taken up by a person's conditioned response performance is specific to the situation. It is necessary to know not only if general factors of conditionability exist but also how large a role such factors play in any actual conditioning situation. It should be noted that in the investigation of individual differences in the conditioning of any one reflex the question of a general factor of conditionability need be of no great practical consequence, nor need it necessarily impinge upon the use of laboratory tests of conditioning for certain predictive purposes.

Turning to a slightly different topic, we all know that extinguished symptoms sometimes spontaneously re-emerge. In whom is this more likely to occur and why? I will attempt to answer the first, and more empirical, part of this question now and leave the "why" until later. In one recent experiment, normal subjects were all conditioned to the same criterion, using the eye blink as the response and a tone as the conditioned stimulus, then extinguished to this same criterion. Twenty-four hours later they were retested for spontaneous re-emergence of the conditioned response. As Figure 1 shows, the good conditioners—those who required fewer reinforcements to condition to the criterion and more repetition of the conditioned stimulus to extinguish—showed *less* spontaneous re-emergence twenty-four hours later. The poor conditioners showed the more immediate spontaneous re-emergence. This is contrary to superficial expectation but consistent with theoretical expectation, as I shall demon-

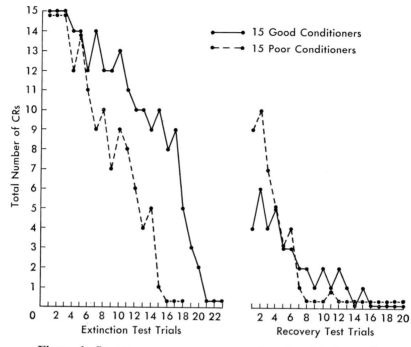

Figure 1. Spontaneous re-emergence of extinguished conditioned eye-blink responses 24 hours after apparent extinction.

strate shortly. This finding, which is merely one example of the more general phenomenon of reminiscence, provides a most interesting lead for clinical research: Could it be the poor conditioner who is more likely to exhibit greater spontaneous remission or return of extinguished symptoms? Note, however, that even though the poor conditioner does show greater initial re-emergence, he also re-extinguishes much more rapidly. Does this mean that in therapy the ready extinguisher may indeed exhibit greater spontaneous remission or symptom return, but that this remission is likely to disappear very readily? Perhaps the good conditioner is the one who should be given depressant drugs when he shows any sign of spontaneous re-emergence of the symptoms, because such activity, although relatively slight, is likely to persist (Franks, C. M., 1963).

DRUG EFFECTS

It is known how a wide variety of pharmaceutical agents affect the formation and retention of classical conditioning responses in man.

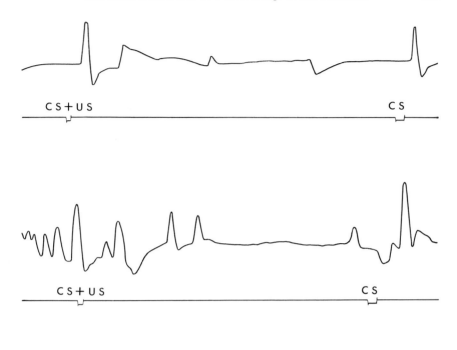

Figure 2. Some typical photoelectrically recorded conditioned eye blinks. The US is an air puff delivered to the right eye and the CS a 1000 cps tone delivered by earphones. In the first instance the US and the CS are presented together. After repeated reinforcements the CS alone produces an eye blink. In the first example there is very little spontaneous blinking. In the third example there is much.

Stimulant drugs, such as amphetamine or caffeine, facilitate the formation and retention of conditioned responses, whereas depressants, such as alcohol, amytal, the bromides, and certain tranquilizers, make the formation and retention of such responses more difficult (Figure 3). In certain cases it is probably not so much the actual ability to *form* central connections which is impaired but more the ability to *utilize* these formed

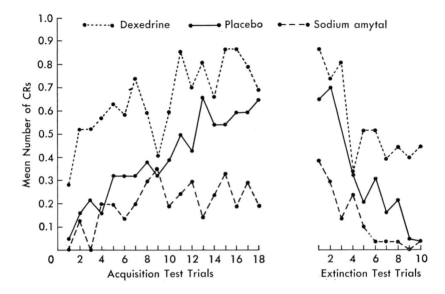

Figure 3. Mean number of conditioned eye-blink responses given at each test trial by groups of normal female subjects after receiving dexedrine, placebo, or sodium amytal.

central connections in actual performance. Thus, when the effect of the depressant or tranquilizing agent wears off, the conditioned response appears with apparently renewed vigor. The implications of such findings for those who wish to employ drugs in behavior therapy—or indeed any kind of psychotherapy, which can also be viewed as an exercise in learning theory—are obvious and require no elaboration here.

It is interesting to note the sometimes apparently paradoxical effects of these drugs upon the ability to form and maintain certain conditioned responses. For example, a large dosage of amphetamine, given to a certain type of person (it will be seen later that this type is the introvert or excitatory dominated person) *initially* does *not* augment the formation—or at least the performance—of conditioned responses. At first, it apparently drastically curtails the performance, and it is only after sufficient time has elapsed that the expected facilitation effect is observed. This phenomenon may perhaps be accounted for in terms of the Pavlovian concept of temporary protective inhibition, according to which central nervous tissue protects itself against excessive excitation by the introduction of a state of temporary inhibition. So it would appear that, when using drugs as adjuncts to therapy, dosage is of importance for reasons additional to those rightly considered to be relevant by the pharmacologist and the physician.

NORMATIVE DATA

Conditioning has been shown to be possible over the gamut of the phylogenetic and ontogenetic scales, from simple snaillike creatures to man, from the fetal stage to the geriatric (Franks, C. M., 1958). But it is usually not possible to make very meaningful inter- and intraspecies comparisons because, even in those instances in which the same reflex arcs have been studied by different investigators, the actual techniques and experimental details usually vary considerably. Pavlov, unlike many of his contemporary psychologists, was always aware of the probable importance of species differences in the phenomena he was studying, and frequently cautioned against the uncritical and premature transfer of conclusions from one species to another. Man is clearly the best subject for obtaining data from which to infer about human behavior but, failing this, it is probably true that the subhuman primates are, with certain exceptions such as some genetic research, the best alternative. It is surprising that, although nonprimates of almost every variety have been studied, comparatively little attention seems to have been given to studies of conditioning in subhuman primates. The fact that very many important experiments have been carried out on more primitive animals only partly limits their value, since there is considerable experimental evidence to suggest that the general laws of cortical functioning derived from animal studies apply also to man (see Franks, C. M., 1958).

It is impossible to develop a systematic application of conditioning to therapy without some normative and developmental data pertinent to those ubiquitous parameters of species difference—age, sex, and intelligence. Despite the universality of these parameters, remarkably little systematic and substantial information is available.

The relationship between age and conditioning is unclear; it is probably one specialized aspect of the general relationship between age and the development of central processes. For example, in certain animals the ability to resist severe stress without becoming "neurotic" (or, if "neurotic," the ability to recover) is a direct function of age. It is often assumed that unequivocal sex differences in conditioning exist, but there are few data available to substantiate this belief. It may well be that such sex differences do occur, but only under certain circumstances, such as the accompaniment of reassuring or apprehension-arousing instructions.

Over the normal range of intelligence, no relationship between conditioning and intelligence has been consistently demonstrated. As far as mental defectives are concerned, the literature, especially in the languages of Western Europe, is sparse and subject not only to the above limitations but, also, in many cases, to those obtaining from poor laboratory techniques, inadequate experimental design, and small numbers. It is there-

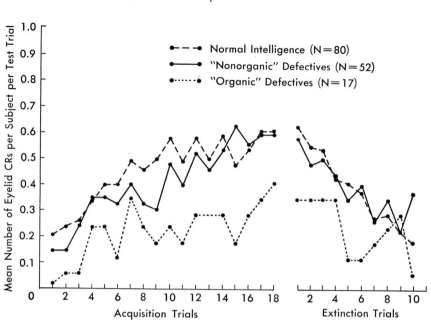

Figure 4. Conditioned eyelid response patterns of subjects of normal intelligence, and of mental defectives with and without any apparent neurological impairment.

fore not surprising that the conclusions are conflicting, with most workers reporting that defectives form conditioned responses more slowly and more poorly than normals, and others arriving at the opposite conclusion. There is apparently fair agreement that congenital idiots form conditioned responses with great difficulty if at all (Franks, V., 1959).

In a recent series of studies of mental defectives it was demonstrated that conditionability, at least as far as the conditioned eye blink is concerned, is related *not* to intellectual differences as such but to neurological differences. Non–brain-damaged normal subjects and *apparently* non–brain-damaged mental defectives condition and extinguish equally well. But brain-damaged mental defectives condition significantly more poorly than non–brain-damaged subjects, be they defective or normal (Figure 4). This point is extremely important because of the widespread but erroneous belief, commonly held and commonly misapplied in both training and therapy with mental defectives, that all mental defectives are intrinsically inferior in conditionability. The applications for behavior therapy with defectives are again self-evident. Further evidence that, when the variable of *obvious* central nervous system deficit is excluded, conditionability is unrelated to intelligence in mentally defective subjects is presented in Figure 5, where, in a group of 52 "nonorganic" mental

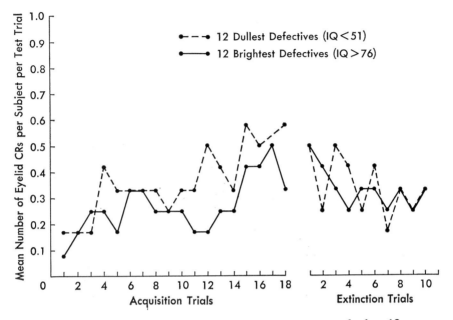

Figure 5. Conditioned eyelid response patterns of the 12 brightest and the 12 dullest "nonorganic" mental defectives.

defectives, the conditioning curves of the 12 brightest (I.Q. over 75) and the 12 dullest (I.Q. under 51) are compared.

There has been interesting Soviet work in this area. It has been focused on an instrumental type of conditioning, and is mainly involved with the "second signal system" and the ability of mental defectives to make verbal connections (Franks and Franks, 1960). It appears that the "second signal system" in defectives involves a more complicated type of connection than that of the simple stimulus-response arc. With respect to this latter type of conditioning, there is no good theoretical reason for expecting low intelligence *in itself* to be associated with poor condition-ability and there was, until recently, little adequate experimental evidence either way (Franks, V., 1959).

INDIVIDUAL DIFFERENCES IN PERCEPTUAL AND MOTOR PERFORMANCE

So far we have discussed a number of empirical findings pertaining only to the conditioned response. But, as already observed, conditioning is but one technique in the task of understanding the principles of central functioning. A variety of additional perceptual and motor tasks is now available for differentiating introverts from extraverts, the effects of stimulant drugs from the effects of depressant drugs, and brain-damaged from non–brain-damaged subjects, and so on. All these tasks, including conditioning, should fit into the same framework if they are manifestations of one underlying principle. Before discussing this framework and showing how many of the results so far merely described on an empirical basis were actually derived beforehand and predicted in terms of the rationale about to be described, I should like to mention some of the techniques, other than conditioning, which are now available. These include the pursuit rotor, sedation threshold, Archimedes spiral, ambiguous figures, tests of vigilance, kinesthetic afterimages, time estimation, visual imagery, performance decrement, speed-accuracy ratios, involuntary rest pauses, reminiscence phenomena, and perception of the vertical.

The clue to individual differences in performance on tests such as these is believed to lie in the properties of the two central processes of *excitation* and *inhibition* which are presumed to underlie all higher nervous activity. And, as has been indicated, recent work in brain physiology tends to confirm the reality of these processes. Along with certain other colleagues, notably Eysenck (1957), excitation and inhibition, and especially the delicate balance of the two, are viewed as constitutional features of the individual which, in their simplest forms, predispose him to develop either excitatory potentials particularly strongly and inhibitory potentials particularly weakly, or else to develop inhibition potentials particularly strongly and excitation ones rather weakly. This powerful concept can be used to develop a tremendous variety of testable predictions about behavior at all levels—in the laboratory, in social situations, and in the therapist's office. One necessary additional assumption is that "inhibition" refers not only to a constitutional or basal and more or less enduring property of nervous tissue but also to some *reactive* property of nervous tissue to stimuli. This concept, developed by Hull and modified by Eysenck, assumes that every response of the organism, whether reinforced or not, brings about an increment of *reactive inhibition*. Reactive inhibition and *basal* inhibition may or may not be closely related.

Individuals with a predominance of basal or reactive inhibition might be expected to behave in a predictable manner during laboratory tests. They should form conditioned responses poorly and extinguish them readily, there should be a much greater decrement in motor performance, and in tasks of vigilance they should be relatively inert in response to stress stimuli.

Stimulant drugs might be expected to alter the excitation-inhibition ratio in favor of excitation, and so facilitate conditioning and make extinction more difficult, whereas depressant drugs or certain tranquilizers might be expected to have the reverse effect (Figure 3). Similarly, brain damage might be expected to impede the conditioning process and facilitate extinction (Figure 4). And protective inhibition is likely to be sooner acquired in a person with innate excitatory dominance who is given a stimulant drug than in a person with inhibitory tendencies.

It becomes possible to account for the fact that *poor* conditioners produce greater spontaneous recovery (Figure 1). The phenomenon of spontaneous recovery of an extinguished conditioned response after an appropriate rest pause is merely an example of the general phenomenon of reminiscence, in which, with no further learning, performance is improved after a rest pause. One explanation of this phenomenon is that during the initial performance reactive inhibition is generated, impairing somewhat the level or quality of the response. During the rest pause the reactive inhibition dissipates and so, upon resumption, there is an immediate improvement, the loss due to forgetting during a short rest pause being usually trivial. Thus, subjects with a predominance of inhibition will condition poorly, extinguish rapidly, show much reminiscence, and then re-extinguish fairly readily.

Eysenck (1957, 1960a, 1960b) has extended this notion into the realm of personality theory by causally linking the personality dimension of introversion-extroversion with its underlying central nervous system substratum, the excitation-inhibition balance. Persons whose central nervous systems are innately prone to excitation rather than inhibition will tend to develop introverted behavior traits and show, in cases of abnormal functioning, dysthymic or introverted neurotic symptoms such as anxiety. Conversely, persons in whom inhibitory potentials predominate will tend toward extroverted behavior patterns and hysteric-psychopathic symptoms. A detailed examination of these postulates cannot be undertaken here, except to point out that from them it is possible to make testable predictions about the relationships between personality variables and performance on such tests as conditioning and reminiscence. Again, the implications for behavior therapy or psychotherapy based upon learning principles are obvious. The hope is that, eventually, the suitability of any one patient for behavior therapy, his likelihood of responding quickly, and the circumstances under which such therapy is most likely to be successful may be predicted by making the appropriate laboratory tests beforehand, and by observing his relative position on the introversion-extraversion continuum.

Neural satiation is a central process which has been introduced to account for individual differences in a variety of perceptual phenomena, such as fluctuation in perspective, visual and kinesthetic figural after-effects, flicker fusion, apparent movement phenomena and perception of the vertical. Satiation, which is, in a sense, the inverse of the Klein and Krech (1952) concept of cortical conductivity, has many points of similarity with reactive inhibition. If this be so, then the general theory which relates inhibition, and hence extraversion, to performance on motor tests can be extended to the perceptual field, and similar predictions may be made relating introversion-extroversion and those supposed to be bad or good satiators to their performance on a wide range of perceptual tests. In a similar manner, the effects of drugs, or brain damage, may be predicted and, hopefully, a new area of techniques becomes potentially available for application in behavior therapy and for predicting the outcome of such forms of therapy.

RESEARCH ISSUES

Despite a good many unknowns, an impressive body of knowledge is already available, and conditioning and behavior therapies have been applied most successfully both to the actual treatment of a wide range of behavioral abnormalities and to the selection of suitable candidates for therapy. One area in which such a technique is being developed vigorously is that of conditioned aversion therapy for the treatment of alcoholics. Vogel (1959) and her fellow psychologists in Ontario are developing techniques whereby galvanic skin reflex conditionability in the laboratory can be used for the selection of alcoholic patients for treatment. A variety of techniques is available for the conditioned response treatment of a wide range of neurotic and other behaviorally abnormal pathologies (Franks, C. M., 1960). Properly designed devices, if adequately constructed and used in conjunction with a skilled investigation of the total situation, have been shown repeatedly to correct the faulty response of bed wetting in children (or adults) within weeks, and to produce no recrudescence, new symptoms, or other adverse effects.

More broadly speaking, the following observations appear relevant. First, with reference to the physical actuality of Pavlovian processes, hitherto largely demonstrable only by inference and conjecture, it is now claimed (with appropriate documentation) that the techniques of modern electrophysiology and histochemistry are providing direct evidence for the existence of these processes and their properties. This brings nearer the far-distant day when the tissue changes we now induce so laboriously by verbal or other external sensory conditioning stimuli will be brought about by electrochemical processes acting directly upon and in the nervous system.

Second, by extending their applications of conditioning beyond the circumscribed and totally exteroceptive elements of reflex arcs which are usually organismically trivial for modern man, Soviet scientists are developing techniques by means of which the so-called unconscious—hitherto the unchallenged domain of Freud and the "psychodynamic" schools of thought—is rapidly becoming amenable to direct experimental control and explanation within a behavioral framework. This is an extremely important advance, especially in view of the often-repeated gibe that conditioning theory and practice is arid, limited, and, unlike "psychodynamic" formulations, able to contribute little to an understanding of complex behavior and psychopathology outside the laboratory. Interoceptive conditioning, in which either the conditioned stimulus or the unconditioned stimulus or both are delivered directly to the mucosa of some specific internal organ, enables the experimenter to study, reproduce, and modify reactions of which the individual is not directly conscious. Razran has provided concise but explicit accounts of the present state of Soviet knowledge in this area, in which interoceptive conditioning is classified according to the type of reaction conditioned: visceral, skeletal, sensory-verbal (Razran, 1961). Apparently, not only may feelings of anxiety, or its unconscious visceromotor accompaniments, become conditioned stimuli for the production of, say, constipation, but sensations of constipation may equally act as conditioned stimuli to bring about anxiety or abnormal bile secretion or hypertension or, indeed, any other functional disturbance. These relationships may be regarded as equivalent to Freud's so-called primary processes. By a consideration of conscious and unconscious verbal and semantic conditioning, Freudian symbolism and secondary processes may likewise be encompassed within the Pavlovian fold.

Third, and an important outcome of the preceding trend, is the fact that in the USSR techniques are being developed for gaining voluntary control over processes which are usually considered to be involuntary. For example, as long as the subject is able to verbalize the process and understand something of the activity involved, he can be trained to control his own pupillary contractions and expansions by repeating the appropriate signal to himself.

Fourth, advances such as those just described necessitate the possession of specialized medical and physiological skills which the average North American or British student of conditioning does not possess because it is not a part of his training. Those who do possess such skills and for whom the acquisition of such medical techniques is a part of their training, e.g., the gastroenterologist, the urologist, and the internist, are usually not very interested in or oriented toward conditioning. In the Soviet Union, for better or for worse—and probably for both—a Pavlovian orientation permeates almost every branch of medicine and medical research, and equips any medical research worker who is so inclined for this type of research.

It has often been suggested that behavior and conditioning therapies represent purely symptomatic treatment and that this is ineffective in the long run, resulting frequently in recrudescence of the same or alternative symptoms, or in a marked increase in anxiety. Pavlov repeatedly pointed out that man is a complex biological system who utilizes countless numbers of reflexes of all kinds, conditioned and unconditioned, beneficial and harmful. The original cause may once have been a relevant, even a traumatic factor, but, in many instances (such as the majority of cases of bed wetting of nonphysical origin), the original cause no longer has any relevance, and there is every justification for concentrating on what does have meaning—the symptom. In such instances treating symptoms which are not due to physical disease should therefore be encouraged rather than overlooked.

GENERAL CLINICAL IMPLICATIONS

Skinner (1953) has argued that those "psychodynamic" theorists who search for inner "causes" for the maladies of their patients, and shun the treatment of the specific behaviors that are causing these individuals difficulty (because these are only *symptoms*) have set up by now nonexisting entities which are thus impossible to treat. Far from the specific behaviors being merely the result of underlying neuroses, they are the very variables to which these traditional personality theorists must ultimately turn in an effort to explain the underlying conditions that they have postulated, but with which they cannot deal directly. One might add that, in many instances, far from emotional training causing, say, bed wetting, it is the bed wetting that brings about the emotional disturbance. So perhaps, rather than criticizing improvement as being merely symptomatic, one might better regard the disappearance or amelioration of the symptom as in itself one of the major criteria of improvement. Such available evidence as there is tends to suggest not only that symptoms fail to recrudesce but that, on the contrary, the removal of one symptom tends also to facilitate the removal of others by decreasing the patient's over-all anxiety level, improving his personal feelings of well-being, and thus helping him develop in the area of interpersonal relationships. Curiously enough, in one of the few regions where Freudian theory lends itself to making testable predictions it fails to obtain support!

Behavior therapy (conditioning therapy) offers a number of advantages over the more "dynamic" schools. On the practical and utilitarian plane, it seems quite feasible that its effectiveness is greater, and the length of treatment shorter. In view of the shortage of therapists, the increasing need for therapy, and the time-consuming nature of psychotherapy, this is no mean advantage. Unlike psychoanalytically oriented therapy, conditioning therapy need not be restricted to the more verbal, intelligent, and educated members of Western society. It can be applied to the unsophisticated, the uneducated, the primitive, the dull, and even to the stranger in our midst who knows no tongue other than his own. There is no longer any need to select cases in terms of verbal, educational, or intellectual efficiency. On the methodological level, the principles can be deduced from learning theory, examined in the laboratory by making experimentally testable deductions, and subjected to clinical test at every phase. In certain instances, it is even possible to manipulate in a controlled and predictable manner the behavior under study. An inevitable and important corollary of these advantages is that a disciplined body of knowledge may eventually arise which can be taught in a systematic manner; students can then be trained as scientists rather than given the mystique of an art. It is, of course, recognized that nonpsychodynamic behavior therapy cannot function without the development of a nonpsychodynamic "behavior diagnosis" in which behavioral description is substituted for speculation and the postulation of dubious entities.

It is premature to give the impression that all of the problems of psychotherapy are on the point of being solved. Much remains to be investigated, and it is quite possible that, as carefully controlled investigation proceeds, the picture will differ vastly from that which our present state of knowledge leads us to accept. Nevertheless, it seems impossible to overlook the fact that a number of working and "proven" techniques are in existence and demand the attention of clinicians and researchers alike.

REFERENCES

EYSENCK, H. J. *The dynamics of anxiety and hysteria.* London, Routledge, 1957.

EYSENCK, H. J. (Ed.) *Experiments in personality.* Vols I and II. London: Routledge, 1960a.

EYSENCK, H. J. A rational system of diagnosis and therapy in mental illness. In L. E. Abt and B. F. Riess (Eds.), *Progress in Clinical Psychology* Vol. IV. New York: Grune & Stratton, 1960b.

FRANKS, C. M. Some fundamental problems in conditioning. *Acta Psychol.*, 1958, *14*, 223–246.

FRANKS, C. M. Conditioning and abnormal behavior. In H. J. Eysenck (Ed.), *Handbook of abnormal psychology*. London: Pitman, 1960.

FRANKS, C. M. Ease of conditioning and spontaneous recovery from experimental extinction. *Brit. J. Psychol.*, 1963, *54*, 351–357.

FRANKS, V. *An experimental study of conditioning and learning in mental defectives*. Unpub. Ph.D. Thesis, Univ. Lond., 1959.

FRANKS, V., & FRANKS, C. M. Conditionability in defectives and in normals as related to intelligence and organic deficit: The application of a learning theory model to a study of the learning process in the mental defective. In B. W. Richards (Ed.) *Proceedings of the London Conference on the Scientific Study of Mental Deficiency, 1960*. Dagenham, England: May & Baker, 1962.

KLEIN, G. S., & KRECH, D. Cortical conductivity in the brain-injured. *J. Pers.*, 1952, *21*, 118–148.

RAZRAN, G. The observable unconscious and the inferable conscious in current Soviet psychophysiology: Interoceptive conditioning, semantic conditioning, and the orienting reflex. *Psychol. Rev.*, 1961, *68*, 81–147.

SKINNER, B. F. *Science and human behavior*. New York: Macmillan, 1953.

VOGEL, M. Alcohol, alcoholism, and introversion-extraversion. *Canad. J. Psychol.*, 1959, *13*, 76–83.

DISCUSSION

Question: I'd like to ask Dr. Franks to make a comment in reference to Razran's article on making the unconscious observable. You referred to that article, and I was puzzled by the whole concept of making the unconscious observable by studying interoceptive conditioning, because it seemed to me that this was similar to making, let's say, Thor's hammer visible in our modern electronic investigations. I wonder if you would comment on whether we are making the unconscious visible, or whether we are making it wither away?

Franks: The question, I think, "unconsciously" has an unfortunate connotation, and this is what happens when we transfer terminology from one field to another. I think we can avoid confusion by speaking of "that which is not directly in the conscious." As you say, the use of the word, "unconscious" doesn't add anything, and may be deceiving. If one is trying to make analogies or comparisons between the two theories, you have to use the language of one or the other.

Question: I would like to ask Dr. Franks if he could comment further on the relationship of autonomic conditionability and capacity to learn instrumental conditioned responses in predicting response to psychotherapy. I would like to ask also if he could comment on the role of autonomic conditioning and of instrumental learning in the psychotherapy process.

Franks: Regarding autonomic conditioning and psychotherapy, I think that much of neurosis can very readily be explained in terms of conditioned autonomic reactions, conditioned emotional reactions, or some related terms. It seems to me to be far easier to explain in these terms than in terms of either plain "conditioning" or something of that sort.

I would have thought the question could have been put the other way around—what has central nervous system conditioning to do with psychotherapy? As Gantt has shown, in cardiac conditioning the central part dies out much faster than the autonomic, and the autonomic part of the conditioning persists. If you have a conditioned response covering many modalities, you find that the central part gets extinguished very rapidly, and the autonomic part is the one that remains and persists. This is Liddell's classic, and, I think, extremely clear finding.

IV

Prospects

CONDITIONING THERAPIES, LEARNING
THEORY, AND RESEARCH

L. J. Reyna, Ph.D.

Having fostered the development of Wolpe's interest in Hullian behaviorism, having presented him in 1947 with the first cat for his laboratory studies on the acquisition and reversal of experimental neuroses, having referred to him his first patient for reciprocal inhibition therapy, and then exchanged appraisals of his developments through the intervening years, I think I must claim a special perspective, together with an intimacy that I hope is not excessively partisan.

The somewhat wide ranging array of topics covered in this book may appear more cohesive if placed in the broader context of experimental psychology. In conditioning therapies[1] a new area of applied experimental psychology is emerging. Laboratory studies of learning, perception, and motivation have been used for some time for devising training and operational procedures, for equipment design, and for programmed instruction.

The inclusion of psychotherapy among the applications of experimental psychology makes sense, if in psychotherapy, as in other areas, the major objective is to make the performance of certain behaviors more efficient and effective. Psychotherapy can be viewed as a set of procedures designed to eliminate a variety of emotionally disturbing responses and useless, undesirable behaviors and to create more efficient behaviors for coping with designated everyday tasks, persons, and situations.

The present paper will examine some assumptions contained in the current use of conditioning therapies, and their implications for research. These assumptions are largely concerned with behavior therapists' views

---

[1] The expression "behavior therapies" is used interchangeably with "conditioning therapies" and "learning therapies."

of behavior disturbances and of the procedures for altering such behavior. Besides comments on these assumptions, some remarks will be made on certain characteristics of comparative research that may be relevant in determining whether—as is claimed—there is a genuine over-all superiority of learning-theory–derived therapies compared with other current psychotherapies.

The development of the behavior therapies

Before examining some major assumptions in behavior therapy it will prove helpful to examine briefly its historical roots and its emergence as a collection of procedures for relieving distress and altering behavior.

The appearance at this time of therapies based on conditioning and learning studies can be traced to several sources. The application of laboratory findings from the psychology of learning to behavioral disturbances began almost immediately following the work of two of its pioneers, Thorndike in the United States and Pavlov in Russia. Early attempts to use learning principles to help relieve emotional distress and nonadaptive behavior were confined to specific problems such as children's fears and bedwetting, and alcoholism. These attempts were based on the belief that behavior problems brought to the therapist are the result of conditioning and that therapy should consist of new learning and/or unlearning. In the meantime, even among some not employing an explicit learning theory approach, therapy had been characterized as a learning process.

In the past fifteen years, growing both out of skepticism toward the claims of psychoanalytic theory and practice, and, paradoxically, out of learning theory translations of analytic therapy accounts (for example, Dollard and Miller, 1950) the influence of learning theory on therapeutic techniques has become more systematic and widespread. This is a logical development, since if therapy is viewed as a learning process, why not deliberately seek conditioning methods?

Thus, conditioning therapies, first inspired by the experiments and theoretical accounts of Pavlov, Thorndike, Watson, Guthrie, Hull, Spence, Skinner, and Mowrer, continued in practice closely to follow laboratory studies and analyses of behavior. (Early applications have been summarized by Hilgard and Marquis, 1940; and more recent ones by Eysenck, 1960; Bandura, 1961; Metzner, 1961; and Rachman, 1963.)

Before long, the therapeutic implications of behavior theory ceased merely to follow laboratory studies and entered into the active development of knowledge of learning and conditioning. This has been true both of earlier studies of experimental neuroses and of more recent studies of fear and avoidance conditioning, conditioning of autonomic reactions, verbal conditioning, and individual differences in conditionability.

A few of these laboratory studies have started from psychoanalytic hypotheses. One may reflect that if the testing of psychoanalytic hypotheses in the laboratory had begun fifty years ago there would not be the sharp distinction found today between "laboratory-derived" and "clinically-derived" therapies. On the other hand, because experimental psychologists were slow to attend to the clinical field, until recently it has only sporadically seen their direct participation. This state of affairs is presently undergoing rapid change. Now the uses of techniques derived from Pavlovian, Hullian, and Skinnerian approaches have become active areas of research.

Two additional developments have made it appropriate to present the challenge of the conditioning therapies at this particular time. With the growth of learning theory, behaviorists' own accounts of a wide range of complex behaviors, particularly relating to personality, adjustment, and psychotherapy, have been steadily increasing (for example: Hull, 1933; Shaffer, 1936; Guthrie, 1938; and Skinner, 1953; for more recent reviews of accounts extending learning principles to complex behaviors see Eysenck, 1961; and Staats and Staats, 1963). And behavior therapies are making their impact now because of their increasing success over a wide range of clinical problems. This last feature is perhaps the most important single immediate basis for the presentation of behavior therapies at this time.

Definition, origin, and maintenance of neurotic behavior

Briefly, the behaviorist regards neurotic behavior as learned behavior: conditioned emotional, verbal, and motor responses have resulted from a history of aversive events and are maintained by immediate reinforcement of behaviors that are instrumental in preventing extinction of conditioned emotional responses. These responses may constitute a small or large part of the individual's repertoire, depending on whether acquired and generalized anxiety responses have led to fresh aversive experiences. In describing the behavior called neurotic as learned, the emphasis is on indicating that this behavior is initially the result of various external operations such as reinforcement, generalization, and contiguity rather than on postulated unobservable inner forces. Accordingly, no underlying disease or state of neurosis is assumed to be present of which behaviors are the symptoms. Rather, behavior that is ineffective, useless, incapacitating, and persistent and that includes strong aversive emotional components may be called "neurotic" or "unadaptive."

In the acquisition and maintenance of neurotic behavior, the role of conditioning and reinforcement, rather than of instinctual processes, is emphasized. Purposive or teleological accounts are avoided in favor of accounts stressing the external and identifiable internal conditions controlling behavior. Early experiences are regarded as relevant to contemporary behavior only insofar as contemporary conditions evoke either the conditioned or the unconditioned components of these experiences. No rigid stages of behavioral development are assumed that make the individual inevitably vulnerable to emotional disturbances.

Goals of therapy

The relief of suffering through reduction and elimination of overt behavior and emotional states that are unadaptive (persistently aversive to self and others) is the prime objective of behavior therapy. "Reorganization of personality" and self-knowledge are not viewed as major objectives or as causal factors in the relief of suffering. Behavior therapies emphasizing manipulations of eliciting stimuli and autonomic responses incompatible with fear or anxiety, are predominantly concerned with eliminating behavior and emotional states that are inappropriate and distressful to the individual. On the other hand, behavior therapies emphasizing operant procedures are predominantly concerned with creating (shaping) behavior formerly absent from the individual's repertoire. The first set of techniques (respondent, Pavlovian-Hullian) have largely been employed for neurotic behaviors, while the latter techniques (Skinnerian) have been used mainly for psychotic, autistic, delinquent, or retarded behaviors.

While the immediate objectives of these two groups of procedures are distinguishable, it would be incorrect to suggest that (a) the processes of eliminating old behavior and of creating new behavior are mutually exclusive, or (b) that changing autonomic behavior has no consequents for skeletomuscular behaviors or the converse, or (c) the procedures employed by these two approaches are confined to classical conditioning or to operant techniques.

The methods for altering behavior

In behavior therapy, the therapist not only explains therapy in learning terms, but explicitly devises, adapts, and utilizes a variety of laboratory techniques to bring about the alteration of conditioned emotional responses and/or behavior. Briefly, using the respondent approach, the therapist looks for the *situations* that elicit the distressing emotional states and proceeds to make these stimuli unable to elicit them. In the operant approach, the therapist focuses on the *behavior* that is desirable and proceeds to increase the probability of occurrence of that behavior. In the account that follows the relevance of methods for altering behavior in respondent therapies is emphasized, since their relevance to operant approaches has been discussed earlier (Bachrach, Chapter 5). Thus, in those instances in which unpleasant conditioned emotional reflexes are present, therapy consists of reconditioning. Just as neutral stimuli can acquire conditioned aversive properties when paired with unconditioned aversive stimuli, conditioned aversive stimuli can become either neutral or conditioned positive stimuli when paired with stimuli evoking a non-aversive, stronger, incompatible unconditioned or conditioned response.

Re-living of original emotional experiences is not viewed as a necessary procedure, nor is knowledge of the historical antecedents of current behavior—in the sense of knowing how original events came to call out certain responses—deemed necessary. Behavior therapists assume that current controls of behavior are identifiable and manipulatable, and that these contemporary stimuli and the behaviors consequent upon them are all that need attention in the treatment of neurotic behavior. (The behavior therapist, like other psychotherapists, takes care to rule out abnormal organic or physiological factors.)

Behavior therapy is openly directive in procedure and in intent. The behavior therapist expresses this when he explicitly defines the goals of therapy, and then arranges conditions so as to alter emotional responses to indicated situations.

The major procedures found in the laboratory that result in diminishing or eliminating current behavior are:

Adaptation-habituation: rapid repetition of the stimulus and/or response, whether reinforcement is present or not.

Extinction: omission of the unconditioned stimulus or reinforcement that previously followed eliciting stimuli or instrumental responses.

Punishment: the introduction of an aversive stimulus following the response.

Counterconditioning: a generic term covering a variety of procedures for conditioning another, incompatible or antagonistic response to the conditioned or discriminative stimulus. Counterconditioning procedures may include direct reinforcement of the incompatible response prior to, along with, or following use of any or all of the three procedures above for the behavior to be eliminated.

Some other labels referring to the variety of conditioning procedures used to alter behavior include: negative practice, discrimination training, methods of toleration, reward training, substitution, response-prevention, stimulus-flooding, and desensitization. Any one of the four classes of methods above, or modifications of them—and sometimes all of them—are employed when the immediate objective is to eliminate conditioned emotional responses and their behavioral by-products.

The most systematic account of the use of conditioning techniques for therapeutic purposes has been presented by Wolpe (1948, 1958). He employs various combinations of anxiety-response–reducing procedures with the aim of achieving counterconditioning—these constituting his techniques of reciprocal inhibition. He endeavors to eliminate the disturbing emotional components of behavior by having their eliciting stimuli conditioned to incompatible emotional states, most often the emotional states associated with relaxation, sexual, and assertive responses. By changing the emotional reactions elicited by the relevant stimuli, the occasion for useless ineffective instrumental responses is eliminated. In systematic desensitization (Wolpe, 1958, 1961) an incompatible emotional pattern, relaxation, is induced, and then paired with gradually more intense emotional stimuli until no emotional disturbance is elicited. The result is that both emotional (autonomic) and motor components of behavior are altered.

Despite differences in theory, there are many practical similarities between Wolpe's methods and those of Salter (1944, 1949), who earlier applied conditioning principles to the full spectrum of neurotic behaviors. The Pavlovian bases and derivations of his procedures are largely interspersed among his case histories and it is sometimes difficult to see the point-to-point relationships to their theoretical origins. Nevertheless, Salter's case studies show a wide range of techniques, which include "excitation" and the external instigation of a variety of assertive and relaxation responses incompatible with previous behaviors.

A broad range of research issues is immediately apparent in the various assumptions of behavior therapies. For example, as noted earlier, conditioning therapies direct their procedures principally to current sources of emotional responses. While knowledge of early history can assist in identifying what the current controls of behaviors might be, neither recall nor re-living of early emotional experiences is found necessary. These, it should be noted, appear to be the most time-consuming features of orthodox analytic therapy (and ones which often produce emotional distress and other unpleasant side effects).

Furthermore, a key procedure in treating patients in whom emotional reflexes (anxiety, depression, panic) are a central feature is the deliberate and controlled introduction of incompatible emotional states and behaviors. Which of these techniques, or combinations of them, and when, and for what kinds of patients and behavior, are most effective? Can drugs be employed to accelerate and maintain relaxation? This brings up questions related to Skinner's analyses of how certain operants can prevent certain respondents. Research and analyses of the sources of reinforcement in therapy are immediately necessary. In all of the foregoing studies, it is clear that direct electrophysiological measures of autonomic and small skeletomuscular responses during the course of treatment claim top priority in those behavior therapies emphasizing counterconditioning of respondents.

The present status of conditioning therapies

It was noted earlier that the effectiveness of behavior therapy over a wide range of clinical ("neurotic") problems was perhaps the most immediate constituent of the present challenge. But to be able to claim successful results merely brings behavior therapy to a level reached by other therapies. To be significant it is necessary to show more than this. The use of these therapies has revealed one outstanding feature which, more than anything else, affords a justification for the present challenge. That feature is the *length of time in therapy.* Time in learning therapies is considerably less than in psychoanalytic therapy (Wolpe, 1958; Eysenck, 1961; Rachman, 1963). At present, "time in therapy" (more accurately, number of hours) is the only available criterion with uniformly acceptable objective status for comparing different therapies. Now the goal of therapeutic practice is to achieve effects in the least amount of time. From this it follows that if the same effects are achieved by either of two procedures, other things being equal, that procedure is to be preferred which requires less time. Obviously, the important implications for research are contained in the expressions: (1) "other things being equal" and (2) "the same effects."

Research on therapeutic subject-matter

Let us consider the question "other things being equal." Early criticism of conditioning therapies was that they were definitely effective only in relatively mild emotional disturbances or in small, isolated or restricted aspects of behavior. The validity of this criticism was apparent in the 1920's and the 1930's. However, in the past two decades published reports on the range and severity of disorders treated by learning therapies reveal the growth of these therapies (Eysenck, 1960, 1961). This growth, of course, owed much to the broadening range of studies undertaken in the laboratory. At the same time the devising of techniques for utilization of this knowledge in the therapeutic situation cannot be overemphasized.

While published reports do not support the view that the variety and severity of "disorders" treated by learning therapists and by psychoanalysts are different, there exists no real evidence that the variety and severity of the cases treated by the two approaches *are not* different. This impasse arises in part from the fact that the two approaches view the patient in different ways. The analyst views the observable behavior of the patient as "symptoms" that are the resultants of various inner forces. "Severity" of disturbance, therefore, is expressed in terms of the nature and state of the hypothesized "inner forces," but these permit comparison only if their behavioral correlates are made explicit. For learning therapists, the problem *is* behavior, behavior that is useless, ineffective, unadaptive, and includes strong emotional (autonomic) reactions. "Severity" for the behavior therapist is expressed in terms of the intensity and pervasiveness of the emotional components of behavior, and of the extent to which the individual's behavior interferes with his performance of daily activities (unavoidable or desired) and with his interpersonal relations. In the same way, comparison of the *varieties* of behavior treated by the two approaches can only be made to the extent that both groups report behavior.

Thus, the behavior therapist has the clear-cut and objective advantage in giving primacy to behavior. But this is only the beginning. Laboratory and clinical research, now and in the future, on the laws of learning will continue to clarify and refine conditioning relationships, and therefore yield potentially more effective techniques of therapy. Accordingly, the evaluation of the effectiveness of present and future *applications* of these laws can profit considerably by specifying and measuring the behavior present at the beginning of therapy. This aspect was brought out by Bachrach (pp. 64ff.) and by Lang (pp. 39ff.). The advantage of such initial assessments and tests of behavior are important for several reasons.

1. A baseline is established against which outcome and follow-up assessments can be compared.

2. Continuous measures of behavior during therapy can provide information on the effects of various procedures, allowing identification of the controlling variables—whether the variables are deliberate or accidental. The desirability of continuous assessment of behavior is implicit in all learning therapies—a feature fully realized and implemented by Jacobson (1938) through his extensive electrophysiological studies of his own variety of learning therapy.

3. Comparisons afforded by these assessments (measures of behavior) provide a basis for deciding on the suitability of different therapeutic procedures for different behaviors. In the design of studies evaluating therapeutic processes and outcomes, the necessity of an untreated control group is diminished in proportion to the extent that the variables manipulated during therapy lead to definite and predictable changes in behavior.

Research comparing the effects
of different therapies

Whether "the same effects" are yielded by different therapies can be compared in terms of (1) outcome on conclusion of treatment, (2) time in therapy, (3) permanence of outcome, and (4) "side effects." Thus far, relatively few remarks have been made about the last two classes of criteria.

One allegation about conditioning therapies has been that their results are temporary or superficial. Recent evidence contradicts this criticism. Some of the evidence to the point, from follow-up studies, has been mentioned by Wolpe (pp. 13–14). I would like to examine some research implications of the question of permanence of "cure"—behavior change and reduction of disturbing emotional states. For the learning therapist, the durability of behavior change is a matter of first identifying the conditions that control the unwanted behavior; and, having identified them, of proceeding to change the conditions that occasion this behavior or to have these conditions lead to other, more desirable behavior. If neurotic instrumental responses and emotional states were to recur, two aspects of the situation would be surveyed: (1) All the factors controlling behavior in the particular conditions surrounding the behavior episode and the state of the individual at the time of recurrence would be examined. (2) The procedure(s) that had been employed for altering or eliminating behavior would be reviewed. Thus, major research efforts must be devoted to techniques and procedures (a) for identifying (within and outside the clinical situation) the variables controlling or influencing behavior, and (b) for identifying the individual characteristics of the patient that make him differentially susceptible to various procedures.

The nature of side effects—such as increased emotional distress and the disruption of interpersonal relationships, working habits, and education—has not hitherto been fully considered among evaluative criteria in comparative studies. In future studies, the nature and extent to which these side effects are present should be clearly specified. Other things being equal, the procedure of therapy that least increases the distress of the individual is to be preferred.

Prospects

Implicit in these research questions is the expectation that more rigorous applications of the laws of learning will render conditioning therapies even more effective; and will extend their use to a broader range of behavior problems (for example, to psychoses, at least as an adjunct to somatic therapies). Future research in the laboratory and in behavior therapy settings should yield improved methods that will take less time, cost less and produce minimum side-effects.

One significant research advantage in behavior therapies is that the behavior therapist does not require for his procedures a strictly private situation, and his observations can therefore be corroborated. Furthermore, at certain stages of therapy, it is even feasible to use substitute therapists —a feature that allows comparative studies of therapists with differing skills and personalities. It is predicted that in the conditioning therapies the identity of the therapist will prove to be less important than the nature of the administered procedure. In the meantime, further laboratory studies of counterconditioning and alteration of acquired behavior, and, particularly, studies in therapeutic and laboratory settings which simultaneously follow the course of change of both respondent and operant behaviors in the same organism, appear to be the most immediate requirement for the further development of behavior therapies. As such research increases, it appears likely that the current widespread interest in *interpreting* all the various forms of psychotherapy in terms of learning theory will be followed by a growing interest in deliberately *adapting* and *using* laboratory learning procedures in therapy.

REFERENCES

BANDURA, A. Psychotherapy as a learning process. *Psychol. Bull.*, 1961, *58*, 143–159.

DOLLARD, J., & MILLER, N. E. *Personality and psychotherapy.* New York: McGraw-Hill, 1950.

EYSENCK, H. J. (Ed.) *Behaviour therapy and the neuroses.* New York: Pergamon, 1960.

EYSENCK, H. J. (Ed.) *Handbook of abnormal psychology.* New York: Basic, 1961.

GUTHRIE, E. R. *The psychology of human conflict.* New York: Harper, 1938.

HILGARD, E. R., & MARQUIS, D. G. *Conditioning and learning.* New York: Appleton, 1940.

HULL, C. L. *Hypnosis and suggestibility: An experimental approach.* New York: Appleton, 1933.

JACOBSON, E. *Progressive relaxation.* Chicago: U. of Chicago Press, 1938.

LAZARUS, A. A. The results of behaviour therapy in 126 cases of severe neurosis. *Behav. Res. Ther.*, 1963, *1*, 69–79.

METZNER, R. Learning theory and the therapy of neurosis. *Brit. J. psychol. Monogr. Suppl.*, 1961, XXXIII.

RACHMAN, S. Introduction to behaviour therapy. *Behav. Res. Ther.*, 1963, *1*, 3–15.

SALTER, A. *What is hypnosis?* New York: Richard R. Smith, 1944; Farrar, Straus, 1955; Citadel, 1963.

SALTER, A. *Conditioned reflex therapy.* New York: Farrar, Straus, 1949; Capricorn Books–Putnam's Sons, 1961.

SHAFFER, L. F. *The psychology of adjustment.* Boston: Houghton Mifflin, 1936.

SKINNER, B. F. *Science and human behavior.* New York: Macmillan, 1953.

STAATS, A. W. & STAATS, C. K. *Complex human behavior.* New York: Holt, Rinehart and Winston, 1963.

WOLPE, J. *An approach to the problem of neurosis based on the conditioned response.* M.D. thesis. University of the Witwatersrand, 1948.

WOLPE, J. *Psychotherapy by reciprocal inhibition.* Stanford: Stanford U. Press, 1958.

WOLPE, J. The systematic desensitization treatment of neuroses. *J. nerv. ment. Dis.,* 1961, *132,* 189–203.

A SURVEY OF SOME CLINICAL REPORTS
OF CONDITIONING THERAPY

ASHEM, B.   The treatment of a disaster phobia by systematic desensitization.   *Behav. Res. Ther.*, 1963, *1*, 81–84.

An obsessive fear of atomic attack that had existed for five years had generalized to newspapers and television. Nineteen sessions of systematic desensitization produced complete recovery, maintained at a three-month follow-up.

BENTLER, P. M.   An infant's phobia treated with reciprocal inhibition therapy.   *J. child Psychol. Psychiat.*, 1962, *3*, 185–189.

Deconditioning of a one-year-old girl's fear of water, using absorption with toys as the counter-conditioning response. After a month's treatment "the infant gleefully initiated approach responses toward the formerly phobic object." Recovery had persisted at a six-month follow-up.

BLAKEMORE, C. B., THORPE, J. G., BARKER, J. C., CONWAY, C. G., and LAVIN, N. I.   The application of faradic aversion conditioning in a case of transvestism.   *Behav. Res. Ther.*, 1963, *1*, 29–34.

Faradic aversion conditioning was applied to a case of transvestism of twenty-nine years' duration. The treatment appeared to produce a complete remission, and six months after the end of treatment the patient remained symptom free.

BOND, I. K., and HUTCHISON, H. C.   Application of reciprocal inhibition therapy to exhibitionism.   *Canad. Med. Ass. J.*, 1960, *83*, 23–25.

Marked weakening in exhibitionist urges of twelve years' duration in a twenty-five-year-old man was obtained by systematic desensitization to stimuli conducive to exhibitionism. A two month follow-up revealed no relapse.

CLARK, D. F.   The treatment of monosymptomatic phobia by systematic desensitization.   *Behav. Res. Ther.*, 1963, *1*, 63–68.

A severe phobia for feathers and birds that a thirty-one-year-old woman had had since the age of six was overcome by twenty sessions of systematic desensitization conducted once a week.

COOPER, A. J.   A case of fetishism and impotence treated by behavior therapy. *Brit. J. Psychiat.*, 1963, *109*, 649–652.

A transvestite fetish was treated by aversion therapy, and the impotence by employing the anxiety-inhibiting effects of the sex impulse. In the course of a three-month follow-up there was a consolidation of confidence and of performance in normal intercourse with the wife.

EYSENCK, H. J.   *Behaviour therapy and the neuroses.*   New York: Pergamon Press, 1960.

This book consists mainly of a classified reprinting of most of the articles describing cases treated by conditioning therapy through 1959, and other articles providing theoretical commentary. There are thirty-six papers and a wide array of conditioning methods are described.

JONES, H. G.   The application of conditioning and learning techniques to a psychiatric patient. *J. abnorm. Soc. Psychol.* 1956, *52*, 414–419.

Bladder responses were directly reconditioned in a patient with marked frequency of micturition.

JONES, M. C.   A laboratory study of fear: The case of Peter. *Pedagog. Sem.* 1924, *31*, 308–315 (also in Eysenck, 1960).

This study describes the deconditioning of a child's fear reaction to furry animals by feeding at progressive approximation to an animal, and is the prototype of desensitization methods.

LAZARUS, A. A.   The elimination of children's phobias by deconditioning. *Med. Proc.* (South Africa) 1959, *5*, 261–265 (also in Eysenck, 1960).

This paper describes the overcoming of the phobias of eighteen children by a variety of conditioning techniques in an average of 9.5 sessions per case. There were no relapses at follow-up.

LAZARUS, A. A.   The treatment of chronic frigidity by systematic desensitization. *J. nerv. ment. Dis.*, 1963, *136*, 272–278.

Sixteen long-standing and refractory cases of frigidity were treated by systematic desensitization. Nine were discharged as "sexually adjusted" after a mean of 28.7 sessions. One of the cases is described in some detail.

LAZARUS, A. A.   The results of behavior therapy in 126 cases of severe neurosis. *Behav. Res. Ther.* 1963, *1*, 69–79.

This paper contains a detailed survey of the treatment of 126 cases, and some information about the parent group of 408.

LAZARUS, A. A., and ABRAMOVITZ, A.   The use of "emotive imagery" in the treatment of children's phobias. *J. ment. Sci.* 1962, *108*, 191–195.

A variation of the desensitization technique is described in which certain positive emotions take the place of relaxation as the inhibitor of anxiety. Nine patients, aged seven to fourteen years, were treated by this method. There were seven recoveries after a small number of sessions, and no relapse or symptom substitution was revealed in follow-ups of six to eighteen months. Details of techniques are given for several of the cases.

MALLESON, N.   Panic and phobia. *Lancet*, 1959, *1*, 225–227.

The author describes, with one illustrative case of examination phobia, the sometimes successful effects of repeated presentation of strongly anxiety-eliciting imaginary stimuli.

MEYER, V.   The treatment of two phobic patients on the basis of learning principles.   *J. abnorm. soc. Psychol.* 1957, *55*, 261–266.

This paper recounts the treatment of two phobic cases by *in vivo* desensitization.

NEALE, D. H.   Behavior therapy and encopresis in children.   *Behav. Res. Ther.*, 1963, *1*, 139–149.

Four cases of long-standing encopresis in children were treated by reward of defecation in the toilet. Rapid success was obtained in three of the cases.

RACHMAN, S.   Treatment of anxiety and phobic reactions by systematic desensitization.   *J. abnorm. soc. Psychol.* 1959, *58*, 259–263.

The behavioral analysis and desensitization of several phobic systems in a single patient are presented.

RAYMOND, M. J.   Case of fetishism treated by aversion therapy.   *Brit. Med. J.*, 1956, *2*, 854–856.

A destructive fetish for handbags and perambulators was overcome by presenting such objects in relation to the nauseating effects of apomorphine.

SALTER, A.   *Conditioned reflex therapy.*   New York: Farrar, Straus, 1949; Capricorn Books-Putnam, 1961.

The treatment of fifty-seven cases is described. Of these, twenty-five are reported in detail. A wide variety of conditioning methods is used, with particular emphasis on assertive behavior, relaxation, and counterconditioning. These techniques are used in the treatment of a wide spectrum of personality disturbances such as anxiety, psychopathy, addiction (alcohol and tobacco), and stuttering. Chapters deal with the treatment of psychosomatic disorders, work block problems of the creative, masochism and its manifestations, shyness, homosexuality, and other sexual disorders.

SCHERMANN, A., and GROVER, V. M.   Treatment of children's behavior disorders: A method of re-education.   *Med. Proc.* (South Africa) 1962, *8*, 151–154.

This paper describes the desensitization within a few weeks of phobic reactions in two children, by employing relaxation in relation to graded exposure to real situations.

STEVENSON, I.   Direct instigation of behavioral changes in psychotherapy.   *Arch. gen. Psychiat.* 1959, *1*, 99–107.

The treatment is reported of twenty-one neurotic patients mainly by the instigation of "communicative, assertive, and affiliative responses." Individual descriptions are given of the treatment of four of the patients.

STEVENSON, I., and WOLPE, J.   Recovery from sexual deviations through overcoming nonsexual neurotic responses.   *Amer. J. Psychiat.* 1960, *116*, 737–742.

Fairly detailed accounts are given of the treatment of two cases of homosexuality and one of pedophilia, by training the patients to behave assertively while ignoring the sexual problem. In each case there was an outcome of normal sexual behavior. The recoveries were found to be enduring in follow-ups ranging from three to six-and-a-half years.

SYLVESTER, J. D., and LIVERSEDGE, L. A.   Conditioning and the occupational cramps.   In Eysenck (1960).
This paper reports 39 cases of writer's cramp and related conditions treated by electric shocks in relation to undesired muscle contractions. It extends an earlier report in the *Lancet*, 1955, *1*, 1147–1149.

TAYLOR, J. G.   A behavioral interpretation of obsessive-compulsive neurosis. *Behav. Res. Ther.*, 1963, *1*, 237–244.
This article includes the treatment of a case of trichopilomania of thirty-one years' standing. An inhibition of the hair plucking compulsion was conditioned by instigating the arrest of the commencement of each movement of the patient's hand to her forehead. Recovery was complete in ten days and had persisted fully at a three-month follow-up.

ULLMAN, L., and KRASNER, L. (Eds.)   *Case studies in behavior modification.* New York: Holt, Rinehart, and Winston, 1964 (in press).
Fifty articles, all case reports, on the treatment of neurotic and psychotic behavior by conditioning procedures. A broad sampling of the recent literature.

WALTON, D.   The application of learning theory to the treatment of a case of somnambulism.   *J. clin. Psychol.*, 1961, *1*, 96–99.
A case of severe somnambulism involving violent behavior was treated by training in assertion in appropriate circumstances. Recovery was accomplished in a few weeks, and after two years there was neither relapse nor the appearance of any substitute symptoms.

WALTON, D. and MATHER, M. D.   The application of learning principles to the treatment of obsessive-compulsive states in the acute and chronic phases of illness.   *Behav. Res. Ther.* 1963, *1*, 163–174.
Various conditioning techniques were applied to six cases of obsessive-compulsive neurosis. Apparent recovery was obtained in two of the cases, and in a third on continuing deconditioning following leucotomy.

WALTON, D., and MATHER, M. D.   The relevance of generalization techniques to the treatment of stammering and phobic symptoms.   *Behav. Res. Ther.* 1963, *1*, 121–125.
Successful treatment is described of two cases, one of long standing stammering and another briefer phobic one, through the employment of assertive training and systematic desensitization, and *in vivo* desensitization.

WOLPE, J.   Objective psychotherapy of the neuroses.   *S. African Med. J.*, 1952, *26*, 825–829.
A short account of some behavioral techniques is followed by four illustrative cases—an anxiety state with amnesia, a blood phobia, an obsessional case, and a case of asthma.

WOLPE, J.   Reciprocal inhibition as the main basis of psychotherapeutic effects. *Arch. Neurol. Psychiat.* 1954, *72,* 205–226 (also in Eysenck, 1960, with additions).

This paper outlines seven techniques by which neurotic habits may be deconditioned. Nine illustrative cases are given.

WOLPE, J. *Psychotherapy by reciprocal inhibition.* Stanford: Stanford University Press, 1958.

A detailed account is given of a number of behavior therapy techniques, with special attention to the institution of assertive behavior, systematic desensitization, and the use of sexual responses for cases of impotence. Other methods described are Jacobson's relaxation, the use of carbon dioxide-oxygen mixtures for overcoming "free-floating" anxiety, the conditioning of "anxiety-relief" responses to the cessation of faradic stimulation, anxiety-inhibiting motor responses, and avoidance-conditioning. Eighteen detailed case descriptions are given, covering a variety of syndromes including psychosomatic states, impotence, obsessions and compulsions, stammering, and hysterical states. Out of 210 patients 188 were assessed as apparently recovered or much improved; and out of 45 followed up 2–7 years 44 were as well or better than at the termination of therapy.

WOLPE, J. Isolation of a conditioning procedure as the crucial psychotherapeutic factor: A case study. *J. nerv. ment. Dis.* 1962, *134,* 316–329.

This describes the systematic desensitization of a very severe phobia for laterally approaching automobiles, involving the use of thirty-three hierarchies and the presentation of 1491 individual imaginary scenes. Recovery was complete and maintained at a nine-month follow-up.

WOLPE, J. Behavior therapy in complex neurotic states. *Brit. J. Psychiat.* 1964, *110,* 28–34.

Illustrating this article are three fairly detailed case reports: one involving a patient with many widespread anxiety-arousing stimulus systems, a case of "character neurosis," and a very severe case of "cleanliness obsession."

YATES, A. J. The application of learning theory to the treatment of tics. *J. abnorm. soc. Psychol.* 1958, *56,* 175–182.

This includes an account of the treatment of several tics in one patient on the basis of massed voluntary practice of the tics.

INDEX